Mary,

Thank you for all of your support of Toastmasters!

You're leaving a great legacy!

Kind regards,
Susan Vollmer

LEGENDS
LEADERS
LEGACIES

By

Susan Vollmer

Bootheel Publishing LLC
Fenton, Missouri, U.S.A.
www.susanv.com

Copyright ©2007

This book is dedicated to <u>everyone</u> who wants to make a difference.

Copyright © 2007 by Susan Vollmer
All Rights Reserved, Second Edition

Library of Congress Control Number: 2007900525

Publisher's Cataloging-In-Publication Data

Vollmer, (Miller) Susan, 1961-
(Legends, Leaders, Legacies)
Legends, Leaders, Legacies / Susan Vollmer
Missouri: Bootheel Publishing, 2007

ISBN 978-0-9795233-0-4

1. World history.
2. Leadership.
3. Vollmer, Susan.
4. Activists—Biography.
5. Human rights.

    I. Title
   II. Legends, Leaders, Legacies
  III. William Wallace (Scotland)
  IV. Joan of Arc (France)
   V. José Rizal (Philippines)
  VI. Edith Cavell (England)
 VII. Rosa Luxemburg (Poland)
VIII. Emiliano Zapata (Mexico)
  IX. Michael Collins (Ireland)
   X. Engelbert Dollfuss (Austria)
  XI. Sophie Scholl (Germany)
 XII. Raoul Wallenberg (Sweden)
XIII. Robert Capa (Hungary)
XIV. Martin Luther King Jr. (U.S.A.)
 XV. Faisal ibn Abdul Aziz (Saudi Arabia)
XVI. Stephen Bantu Biko (South Africa)
XVII. Anwar el-Sadat (Egypt)
XVIII. Indira Gandhi (India)
XIX. Yitzhak Rabin (Israel)
 XX. Ahmad Shah Massood (Afghanistan)

Legends, Leaders, Legacies

Table Of Contents

William Wallace (Scotland)	Page 001
Joan of Arc (France)	Page 023
José Rizal (Philippines)	Page 029
Edith Cavell (England)	Page 040
Rosa Luxemburg (Poland)	Page 050
Emiliano Zapata (Mexico)	Page 067
Michael Collins (Ireland)	Page 089
Engelbert Dollfuss (Austria)	Page 108
Sophie Scholl (Germany)	Page 119
Raoul Wallenberg (Sweden)	Page 127
Robert Capa (Hungary)	Page 158
Martin Luther King Jr. (U.S.A.)	Page 181
Faisal ibn Abdul Aziz (Saudi Arabia)	Page 198
Stephen Bantu Biko (South Africa)	Page 213
Anwar el-Sadat (Egypt)	Page 222
Indira Gandhi (India)	Page 249
Yitzhak Rabin (Israel)	Page 268
Ahmad Shah Massood (Afghanistan)	Page 298
Looking At Leaders	Page 317

INTRODUCTION

Sometimes the task at hand seems so formidable that you don't even want to begin. You question whether or not your contributions will be noticed. You question your ability. You question if one person can make a difference.

Not only can you make a difference for good or for bad, but the action you take today or tomorrow could have an effect on history that you may never even realize in your lifetime. No matter what your age is, no matter where you came from or where you will go – you have something to contribute – just like those who came before us.

Here are their stories. . . .

WILLIAM WALLACE

During the time of William Wallace's birth in the 1270s, Scotland was experiencing a time of peace. Even though sources conflict about his birth year, location and even who his father was, there seems to be no doubt of his love of country and belief that no one should be ruled by a foreign oppressor.

King Edward I (Longshanks)
────────────────────────────

Also around the time of William's birth, the current king of England died. His successor was named Edward, and he would become William's and Scotland's greatest nemesis. Edward was in Italy when he received news of his father's death and took his time returning home. He stayed abroad almost a year. He returned to England and became crowned on 18 August 1274 at Westminster. King Edward who was unusually tall for his age received the nickname of "Longshanks."

The Great Cause

In 1286, King Alexander III of Scotland died suddenly when his horse went off a cliff while he was riding at night. He had already outlived all of his children. The next in line to the throne was his four-year-old granddaughter, Margaret, who was living in Norway. Due to Margaret's age, an interim government was created in Scotland.

Margaret, also known as "the Maid of Norway," was being brought to Scotland at the age of eight. King Edward had already obtained approval for her to marry his son at some point in the future. It seemed to be welcomed by the Scottish.

On the voyage from Norway to Scotland, she developed an illness and died. Her body was returned to Norway, and this ended the ancient royal Scottish line. After Margaret's death, 13 more distant relatives came forward to lay claim for the throne. These Scottish nobles asked King Edward to assist in the arbitration. Before the king of England assisted, however, he required that all contenders first recognize him as "Lord Paramount of Scotland."

They all consented. This was committed to in writing and verified by their individual seals. On 11 June 1291, King Edward ordered that all Scottish castles be temporarily surrendered to him until the Scottish throne had been decided. He also demanded that Englishmen replace all of the Scottish officials.

Determining who would be next on the Scottish throne was referred to as "the great cause." Out of those vying for the position, the two leading contenders were John Balliol and Robert the Bruce. The process of establishing a Scot to the throne seemed to be dragging out. King Edward decided he had more important matters to attend to and adjourned the proceedings until 2 June 1292. At that time, it was delayed again until 14 October 1292.

For more than a month, the hearings lasted and finally finished on 17 November 1292. That was when King Edward ruled in favor of John Balliol. He became King John of Scotland before the end of 1292. The concessions that King Edward had already obtained made it difficult to have an independent Scotland.

Becoming An Outlaw

While the Scottish nobility had been fighting over the throne, William Wallace became involved in fights of his own. In December 1291, William became involved in a skirmish with a group of young Englishmen, who wanted to steal his dagger. William killed one of the men, who happened to be the son of the local constable. The English branded William as an outlaw and placed a bounty on his head. He moved in with one of his uncles, Sir Richard, who was an elderly knight who had become blind and disabled from previous fights with the English.

One day in February 1292, while William was fishing for their supper, a group of English soldiers decided they would take his catch. When William offered them half of the amount, it was not sufficient, and a fight broke out. When it was over, William had killed three of the five English soldiers. To the English, William was viewed as a lawless murderer who must be brought to justice. To the Scottish, William was an avenger trying to reclaim what belonged to Scotland. William returned to his uncle's with the horses and supplies from the dead soldiers. Sir Richard was so upset about the deaths that William had to leave. He and a young page rode off to live in the forest.

Robin Hood

William knew he would be put to death if caught by the English. He found refuge in the Leglen Woods located along the River Ayr. Some people believe that the legend of Robin Hood is based on the real life of William Wallace. Operating out of the forest, William not only helped the poor but may have been the first to use what we now call guerrilla tactics.

The Destruction Of Berwick

In February 1296, in the seaport of Berwick, some English merchants were killed. A mob stole the goods stored in their warehouses. King Edward decided to put the Scots in their place by demonstrating an English show of force.

Four English ships entered the harbor. Two of them ran aground and were burned by the Scots. On 30 March 1296, about 5,000 troops on horses and 3,000 soldiers on foot invaded the city. The English overran the town. For three days, the English murdered Scottish civilians, including women and children – even a woman while she was trying to give birth to a child was killed.

An estimated 17,000 to 20,000 Scots were murdered. Some of the corpses were heaved into the sea – others were thrown into huge pits for mass graves. The horror of this large-scale invasion and attack was intensified because the Scots had previously considered the English as friendly allies.

After the destruction of Berwick, King John of Scotland sent a letter on 5 April 1296 to the English court. The letter officially renounced any allegiance to King Edward of England.

England's invasion began the Wars of Scottish Independence, and the Scots would suffer several defeats. On 10 July 1296, King John abdicated his throne. The English imprisoned him in the Tower of London. He and his son later lived under house arrest in papal custody.

Many Scots still viewed him as their rightful king. The next month in August 1296, the Bruce family swore their loyalty to Edward of England. However the following year, the younger Robert the Bruce would participate in a Scottish uprising against England.

Another Fish Fracas

In 1296, William was on the streets of Ayrshire. He observed that an English soldier stopped the sheriff's servant. This same sheriff was also William's uncle. The servant had bought fish at the market and was returning home when the soldier demanded to be given the fish.

William told the soldier to leave the servant alone. The soldier attempted to stab William, and William killed him. English troops converged and overpowered William, taking him to a dungeon. His uncle tried to get him released but to no avail. The gaoler at this English-controlled dungeon gave William only water and rotten herrings to eat. As a result, he developed a fever and then lapsed into a coma, which assimilated death. William's body was then thrown into a dung heap.

News spread quickly of the death of William Wallace. A nurse who had previously taken care of William as a child went and requested the body for burial. She and her friends took the body home and began the cleansing.

She then realized that he was near death but was not dead. She and her family nursed him back to health. At the same time, they arranged a wake to keep the pretense going. Once recovered, he set off for Glasgow. The only weapon he had was a rusty blade. Along the way, he stepped aside to let an English soldier and two yeomen pass. The soldier was suspicious and insisted that William come back to town with them. He could not go back to town and the dungeon, so he killed all three of them, taking their horses and gear.

One of the reasons William did so well in fighting was due to his size. While most men of that time averaged about 5 feet, William towered over them. His height was estimated from 6' 7" to 6' 9" (roughly the equivalent of 2 meters).

He was able to withstand hunger and fatigue better than most. He could live outdoors in inclement weather. Along with his enormous strength, he had a heroic mind. He firmly believed in patriotism to his beloved Scotland. Although he did not own any land and he had no title, many considered his beliefs nobler than the gentry of Scotland. At different times over the years, the Scottish nobles or earls would swear their loyalty to the king of England. They were concerned about preserving their lands and estates both in England and Scotland. William Wallace was the only prominent figure who had "not" sworn any loyalty to the king of England.

Warriors For Wallace

Men literally looked up to William. Not just due to his size, but they looked up to him because he inspired them. After leaving the dungeon prison, William started wearing armor for protection. Through his informers, William learned that an English knight would be traveling through on an important mission. William believed that this man had killed his father. Plus, this knight and his men were transporting treasures stolen from the churches of Scotland, along with other gold and silver.

The English knight had 180 men. William had 50 men. He chose as the place for attack a narrow passage where the English could ride no more than two side-by-side. The Scottish also blocked part of the passage with boulders. William and his men attacked. They thrust their spears and swords underneath the horses where possible. This would force the English soldiers to fight on foot.

Despite having more than three times the number of soldiers, the English seemed to lose their drive after their leaders were killed. About 80 English soldiers escaped, and 100 were left dead on the field. The Scottish lost three men.

William and his men proved that the much-feared armored horsemen could be defeated. The bounty included about 200 packhorses with wine and supplies, weapons, armor and treasures.

Kinclaven Castle

In another skirmish, William's men were about the same number as the English. William's guerilla forces hid in the woods near Kinclaven Castle. As the main group of 90 English cavalry approached, William and his men charged on foot. Again, they mostly went for the horses at their bellies and legs. The disabled horses would throw their riders to the ground, where the soldiers would be attacked.

About 60 English soldiers including the commander died on the field. The remaining troops fled to the castle with William and his men in pursuit. The Scots did not believe in taking prisoners, so the remaining English soldiers were killed. Those who were released included two priests, the women and the children; the Scottish force then burned down the castle.

As a result of the Kinclaven attack, the English gathered a cavalry of 1,000 men and horses. Five units surrounded the woods and a sixth went for direct pursuit and assault. During this skirmish, one of the English archers hit William under the chin with an arrow, which caused a minor injury. The number of Scots by this time had dwindled to 50 men, while the English brought in a re-enforcement of 300. William and his men decided to retreat, and they slipped away. The English went to the city of Perth. The following night William and his men returned and retrieved the Kinclaven booty that had been hidden under the rocks.

William wanted to go to Perth also because he had a mistress there. He went to meet the girl, and they also set up a date for their next rendezvous. The English had recognized him and questioned the girl later who confessed the next designated meeting time.

When William arrived next time, she quickly advised what had transpired. He attempted to dress up like her in a nightgown and cloak, leaving the room and house saying that Wallace is locked in. Two of the guards fell for the ruse, but then two other soldiers became suspicious and pursued him. Still, William and his men slipped away and went to Elcho Park.

Maid Marion

Sometime in 1296, William is believed to have met 18-year-old Marion Braidfute. Her father had died, and she was considered an heiress. She lived in a town house in Lanark. They met in the nearby Church of Saint Kentigern. The local sheriff in the area, William Heselrig, wanted Marion to marry his son.

William fell in love with Marion. He discussed the issue with one of his closest associates, who advised William to marry her. However, William felt that he could not marry and settle down until after he had liberated Scotland. To him, love and war did not mix. He did pledge to come back and marry her after Scotland was free. Sources seem unclear as to whether or not they actually married and whether or not they had a baby girl in April 1297.

In May 1297, William attended service again at the Church of Saint Kentigern. He and his companions were stopped by English soldiers who began taunting him about Marion. Quickly, about 200 English had gathered. William and his companions started fighting and then escaped. They left behind 50 dead and wounded Englishmen. William and his men stopped by Marion's house before leaving for the countryside.

Then, the remaining English went to Marion's house. When they realized that William and his men were no longer there, they smashed the door in. The sheriff had Marion seized and killed right then.

William found out what happened. That same night, he and his men returned to Lanark. They entered through different town gates individually, so that they didn't arouse suspicion. Then they reassembled; William and his men went to the sheriff's home, smashing in his door. Then, William killed the sheriff in his own bed. Their revenge for Marion's death led to 240 Englishmen being killed that night. As usual, the Scots spared the priests, women and children.

The Battle Of Stirling

On 11 September 1297, William and a noble named Andrew Moray joined forces for the Battle of Stirling. Stirling is located in the heart of Scotland on Castle Hill, surrounded by steep cliffs on three sides. It is considered an immense fortress. Stirling and its bridge were known as the gateway to the Scottish Highlands.

One English force was estimated at 50,000-foot soldiers and 1,000 cavalry. Another English force consisted of 8,000 infantry and 300 soldiers on horses. The English Army was an army of conscription, where many had been forced to join. It included not only Englishmen but also Irishmen and those from Wales. Some of the men had also been forced to join by their feudal superiors.

The Scottish forces were composed of a volunteer army. They were enduring the brutal rule and the arrogance of the English occupation. They were ready to sacrifice everything for a change. They had become patriots.

Most medieval wars in the past had involved feudal disputes. The idea of citizens coming together to fight for national unity and identity was a new concept.

The English sent two friars over to see the Scottish forces and offer terms for surrender. The friars returned and said the Scots wanted to avenge and deliver their country. The friars may have overestimated the Scottish forces at 40,000-foot soldiers and 180 cavalry. The English forces started crossing the Stirling Bridge, which would only allow about two horsemen abreast at a time. William and his forces waited while the crossing continued to determine the best time to strike. He wanted to wait and allow as many soldiers over as possible that he thought the Scots could safely defeat.

William blew a single blast from a horn, signifying time for the attack. The Scots descended brandishing their swords and spears with an unleashed fury. They made their way to the bridge and closed it to prevent any more troops from landing. Other troops kept trying to force their way onto the overcrowded bridge. Some of those packed on the bridge, jumped into the water but then drowned from the weight of the armor.

Of the English forces who crossed the bridge and perished that day included nearly 5,000 infantry, 300 archers and 100 cavalry. A few had removed their armor and swam back to the other side.

This was considered a huge victory for the Scots. After the battle of Stirling, William and his top commanders were knighted. From 1297 to 1298, Sir William Wallace was also named Guardian of Scotland. This title designated the head of the state of Scotland.

William decided the next step was to take the battle to English soil. The Scots came upon a monastery in the town of Hexham in northern England. The monks ran from them to take refuge in the ruins of the building. The Scottish soldiers demanded the treasures of the church from the monks. When William entered the monastery, he had the soldiers stop. He then asked the monks to celebrate Mass.

The service proceeded smoothly until William stepped outside of the chapel. Then, his men proceeded to steal everything in use, including the robes of the monks.

William had the three monks stay near him for protection while his other soldiers looted the countryside over the next two days. Before they left, he gave the monks a document granting safe passage in his name. Then, William and his forces invaded the counties of Cumberland, Northumberland and Westmorland.

The English countered by launching a revenge attack on Annandale, a historic district which was located in southern Scotland. Several thousand men descended on the town driving 308 Scots into the swamp. They plundered the town and then went to hit and burn 10 more villages before Christmas 1297. Those who lived in border towns in both countries suffered more than most during the attacks.

During the winter of 1297 to 1298, William moved from a volunteer army to a conscription army to gain more forces. He organized a chain of command based on merit, instead of feudal systems.

William required gallows to be built in every town to serve as a threat to those who didn't sign up for their military service without a proper excuse. He went to Aberdeen to execute those by hanging who had avoided the service.

Battle Of Falkirk

The Scottish nobles remained conspicuously absent by not supporting William and his forces against the English. In July 1298, King Edward himself was leading the English forces. A scout was sent ahead and found the Scottish army was about 18 miles away. The English forces headed out. They camped at nightfall. While the king was sleeping, his own horse stepped on him.

King Edward mounted his horse and said they were moving out, even though it was still dark. They headed out. After the sun had risen, they finally arrived where the Scottish Army was stationed. William seemed to have abandoned his guerilla tactics for more of a standard fight where both sides are expecting the attack.

The Scottish archers did not seem as skilled as the English. Plus, the English had superior equipment with better range and velocity. King

Edward brought his extensive foot soldiers to the attack. Standing back were the Welsh forces. Once they observed that the English were going to win, they joined them. The Scottish infantry was practically wiped out with 10,000 soldiers killed. William and his remaining men retreated to a densely wooded area.

After the defeat at Falkirk, William decided to resign as Guardian of Scotland. Joint guardians were then named, including Robert the Bruce and John Comyn of Badenoch, who was the brother-in-law of the former King John of Scotland.

William left in late 1298 to go to France and request assistance in the struggle for Scotland's freedom. He formed a guard of Scottish exiles in France and fought two battles against the English. He then went to Rome in 1303 to ask for help for Scotland. He returned to his homeland that same year.

In August 1305, a Scottish knight who was supporting the king of England used treachery to help capture William. The knight had his nephew placed as a new page for William.

One evening, while William was sleeping, the new page removed all of William's weapons. Then the page signaled for his uncle Sir John de Menteith to send his men in for the capture.

William's long-term attendant was taken outside where he was stabbed to death. William was captured and taken to Westminster in London for a mockery of a trial.

As typical of law in the Middle Ages, William had no legal rights or privileges. On 23 August 1305 in England's Westminster Hall, the English justices read the list of charges against him. William was not allowed to speak or to defend his actions.

The Sentence
───

Immediately after the indictment was read, there were no witnesses and no deliberations, as in modern justice. Instead, the English went straight to the sentencing.

- William would be dragged through the streets of London.
- William would be hanged until he was almost near death.
- William would be tortured by being disemboweled.
- He would then be decapitated.

- His head would be impaled on the spikes at London Bridge.
- His remaining body would be cut into four pieces and placed in these areas to serve as a warning to all who pass by:
    - Berwick
    - Newcastle upon Tyne
    - Saint Johnston
    - Stirling

The English carried out the execution of William Wallace as described that same day with the hanging and mutilation occurring at Smithfield Market. Instead of serving as a lesson to not challenge the English, the torture of William Wallace reminded the Scottish people what it meant to be ruled by a foreign oppressor. William had given them hope instead of humiliation. He had proven that the English were not invincible. And the Scottish people did not forget what he had started.

Robert The Bruce

Seven months later, the Scottish noble Robert the Bruce declared himself King of Scotland. However, he would still have to fight for his kingdom and for Scotland. King Edward of England continued to invade Scotland. He finally died on 7 July 1307, and then his son Edward II took over.

Robert the Bruce continued the fight started by William Wallace. In 1314, Robert the Bruce and his forces finally won Scotland's independence.

WILLIAM WALLACE (Scotland)

| Born: (estimated) 1270 – 1276 | Died: 23 August 1305 | Age: 29 – 35 |

"Tell your people that we have not come here to gain peace, but are prepared for battle, to avenge and deliver our country. Let them come up when they like, and they will find us ready to meet them."

~ William Wallace

(Reported in the book "William Wallace: Brave Heart")

JOAN OF ARC

In France during the 15th century, the Hundred Years War with the English was taking its toll. In addition to war, the country faced famine and disease. No one, at first, noticed a young farm girl, who couldn't even read. But Joan of Arc had an unwavering conviction in God and a deep-found faith influenced by her mother.

"Saint Michael told me that I must be a good child, and that God would help me. He taught me to behave rightly and to go often to church," as reported in the book "Joan of Arc – In Her Own Words." This is based on her testimony in French court. In addition to Saint Michael, she often had visions of Saint Catherine and Saint Margaret. "The name by which they often named me was Jehanne the Maid, child of god," said Joan.

Civil war erupted in France between various factions. In the winter of 1428, one faction – called the Burgundians – destroyed the home of Joan's family. Her visions spoke to her of saving France.

Divine Influence

Joan maintained that she received direct inspiration from God. The saints told her to help lift the siege of Orléans, chase the English out of France and guide the rightful heir to the throne, the Dauphin Charles, and take him to his coronation. Dauphin refers to the oldest son of a royal family.

With permission from Charles, Joan led his army in 1429, which resulted in the freeing of the city of Orléans. Joan and the army drove the English out of the Loire Valley, and Charles was crowned King of France on 17 July of that same year. That following spring, Joan was captured by the Burgundians who auctioned her off to English captors for 10,000 pounds. The English turned her over to French clerics who had been appalled by her claims of having direct access to God.

The Legal Charges

The French clergy charged her with heresy and witchcraft. Heresy means having a belief that is opposite of the official church view. The actual legal procedure is referred to as an inquisition. This is because instead of having a prosecuting attorney, the judge brings the legal charges against the defendant, which was Joan.

During the trial, Joan was questioned and admonished several times about wearing men's clothing. One time, she replied that she would wear a woman's hood and long robe if she could go to church and receive Holy Communion.

Then after returning to prison, she planned to resume her manly attire. "When I have finished what God sent me here to do, I'll wear women's clothing," said Joan, according to the book "The Trial Of Joan Of Arc."

On 24 May 1431, Joan had been worn down from the trial, which began four months earlier on the 9 January 1431. She recanted her prior testimony and said she would yield to the clergy. She allowed her head to be shaved and dressed in women's clothing. She was sentenced to life in prison.

The following Monday, on 28 May 1431, she wore men's clothing again in her cell. When questioned, she said they had not taken her to Mass as promised, and she felt it more appropriate to wear this clothing.

Joan withdrew her confession. She said she only confessed because of fear from dying by fire. The voices of her saints advised that it was wrong to confess to things she was not guilty of.

The court declared her a relapsed heretic who would be handed over to secular authorities. On 30 May 1431, the judges arrived at the Old Market of Rouen, about 71 miles (114 kilometers) northwest of Paris. A multitude of persons had gathered. Joan was brought out wearing chains. She walked to the market square and saw the pile of wood where she would be torched. She cried. When she asked to have a crucifix held in front of her, a golden one was brought from a nearby church.

The executioner tied her to a stake and set a fire at Joan's feet. Before death, she cried out the name of Jesus multiple times. Her eyes remained steady on the crucifix as the flames consumed her earthly body, and her soul became free.

Retrial

Twenty-four years later in 1455, the pope approved a retrial regarding the case of Joan of Arc. A tribunal of three men convened interviewing more than 100 witnesses from Paris to Rouen to Orléans. On 7 July 1456, the original trial verdict was declared null and void. To celebrate, a copy of the trial's transcripts was burned at the archbishop's palace. Joan's mother was still alive at the time to know her daughter's name had finally been cleared.

In tribute to her sacrifice, the Roman Catholic Church canonized Saint Joan of Arc in 1920. This was 489 years after her death. Joan of Arc is known as the patron saint of soldiers and of France.

JOAN OF ARC (France)		
Born: (estimated) 6 January 1412	Died: 30 May 1431	Age: 19

"Whenever I am unhappy, because men will not believe me in the things that I say at God's bidding, I go apart and pray to God, complaining to him that those to whom I speak do not easily believe me. And when I have made my prayer to God, I hear a voice that says to me: 'Child of God, go, go, go! I shall be with you to help you. Go!' "

~ Joan of Arc

(Reported in the book "Joan of Arc – In Her Own Words")

JOSÉ RIZAL

From the 1500s throughout the 1800s, Spain dominated the Philippines, which served as a colony. The natives of the Philippines, known as Filipinos, were subjected to foreign taxes and forced labor.

All Filipino families and unmarried adults were expected to pay the head tax, which brought great profits to the officials. Another Spanish government fee was known as the falla. A Filipino could be exempted from forced labor by paying the falla. Those who could not afford the fee were forced to work for the foreign government from 16 to 60 years of age. The Filipinos built roads and bridges, worked in shipyards and cut timber for no pay – just a ration of rice.

Downtrodden and humiliated, the laborers did not know anymore what it meant to be Filipino. One person who helped lead the people to a sense of cultural identity was José Rizal.

Francisco Mercado and his wife, Teodora Alonso, had their seventh child in a family of 11 children. He was born on 19 June 1861 and named José. His father leased the land, where he ran a successful sugar plantation. His mother took care of a store, where she sold food like hams and jellies.

His family was not Spanish. They were native people to the Philippines, referred to sometimes as Indios. They lived in one of the nicest homes in the village of Calamba, located on the island of Luzon.

They would often receive visiting Spanish officials in their home. About the same year as José's birth, one officer of a civil guard stopped by and requested food for his horse. José's father unfortunately had no feed for his own animals or any to give away. The officer, who was offended, harbored a grudge for 10 years.

As a result, he later conspired with a woman who falsely accused José's mom of being an accomplice in a plan to poison her. José's mom was arrested for attempted murder when he was 10 and forced to walk approximately 31 miles (50 kilometers) to prison. She would spend two and a half years in prison before she was acquitted.

Other injustices performed by Spanish authorities included:

- Removing Filipinos from their administrative positions.
- Giving noncommissioned officer positions at the navy yard only to the Spanish.
- Making the Filipino shipyard workers start paying taxes, when they were previously exempt.

The workers revolted and more than 200 Filipinos commandeered the fort on 20 January 1872. During the fighting, seven Spanish officers were killed.

In retaliation, the Spanish government arrested three Filipino priests and executed them for treason.

The Importance Of Education

Fortunately, José received many opportunities at education. He not only learned his native language of Tagalog but also Spanish and Latin. His older brother, Paciano, suggested it would be safer for José to use his second surname of Rizal while in school instead of the family name. This might minimize some of the discrimination he would face.

José loved literature and reading. One of his favorite novels was "The Count of Monte Cristo" by Alexandre Dumas. This was the story of a young man who faced many injustices yet fought his way back through education.

José attended the University of Santo Tomas in Manila. However, he wanted to leave the Philippines and study abroad. He knew his parents would object. José pretended to be going on a trip to Manila, but he was really headed on a long journey to Spain – the land of his country's captors.

He left letters for his parents and sisters. He explained that he could not just stay and lead a comfortable life.

> "I would have done nothing worthwhile. . . . I, too, have a mission to fulfill, a life alleviating the suffering of my fellow men."
>
> (Reported in the book "Freedom's Martyr")

In 1882, José moved to Spain where he studied medicine and became Dr. Rizal. He received not only an academic education but a political one as well. He saw the freedoms that the Spanish citizens enjoyed compared to the oppression of the Filipinos back home.

José believed that education could solve the problems caused by inequality. He believed that education could bring freedom.

Before his trip to Spain, he left a poem for a girlfriend named Leonor Rivera, who was also his cousin. Leonor and José considered themselves engaged. But neither of their parents approved of the relationship. Her mother sent her away to school. Then, Leonor became upset that José had left the country without telling her in advance.

José would write Leonor, but her mother intercepted the letters. She finally married a man she didn't love in June 1891. Leonor would later die about two years after her marriage.

Reform Through Writing

Leaving Spain, José continued his studies in Paris and Heidelberg, specializing in ophthalmology and also writing on the side. His first novel completed in 1886 was written in Spanish and titled "Noli Me Tangere" (meaning "Touch Me Not"). The book was a passionate exposé about the evils of the Spanish friars in his home country.

At that time, most publishers printed books in English, French or German. If José wanted his book printed in Spanish, he would need to self-publish it. José would need 500 pesos to print 1,000 copies. He started eating only one meal a day and saving the rest of his money for printing costs. He became malnourished and sick.

A doctor, who was also a friend of José's, offered to help by providing funds. As a result, in February 1887, "Noli Me Tangere" started rolling off the press in Spanish. The book became a success. The Filipino Government banned the book as being subversive. However, it was still smuggled in.

Copies were disguised with different covers to make them appear as a history book or a book of poems. On the 5 August 1887, José returned home. At 26 years of age, he established an eye clinic to treat the residents of Calamba. Some paid in cash, and others bartered with livestock or food.

Nearly six months later, on 3 February 1888, José left his homeland to give his relatives peace. Now, it was his name that was bringing problems from the authorities.

José wrote numerous articles for the Barcelona newspaper "La Solidaridad." José advocated replacing the Spanish friars with Filipino priests, and that Filipinos and Spaniards should be equal in the eyes of the law. He described the Philippines, which existed before the Spanish invasion, giving everyone a truer sense of history and cultural identity. Plus, he wrote about the problems caused by colonialism.

As a sequel to his first book, José self-published another novel by pawning some diamonds that he had to pay for the printing. In 1891, he published the book called "El Filibusterismo," which means "The Subversive." This novel implied that armed revolution might be the only path to effect social change. He dedicated the novel to the three Filipino priests (José Burgos, Mariano Gomez and Jacinto Zamora) who were declared traitors and executed in the Philippines after the shipyard rebellion.

In Exile

In June 1892, José received approval to leave Hong Kong for return to the Philippines. After several visits with José, the governor-general requested and received amnesty for José's family in the Philippines.

In July 1892, José was accused of treason and formulating unrest against Spain. As a result, he was taken to Fort Santiago and held in prison without a trial. He was then exiled to an island south of the Philippines called Dapitan. After his exile, others formed a revolutionary group named the Katipunan.

While in exile, José shared a lottery ticket with the commandant and another Spanish gentleman. They won 20,000 pesos. With his share of the winnings, he sent part to his father and also bought an estate next to the ocean. He built several houses and other buildings. He started a school, continued his medical practice and started farming the land. He planted banana and coconut trees. He created a machine, which made bricks. He then used the bricks in the development of a public waterworks, a fountain and a sanitary drainage system.

In February 1895, José met a young Irish woman named Josephine Bracken when she brought her foster father to see José for vision problems. Josephine was 18 years old at this time when José requested permission from the bishop to marry her. This was denied unless José would retract previous statements made about the Spanish friars.

Civil marriage by the government was not available in the Philippines, so they were unable to marry. As a result, she just lived with him, creating a shock to his family.

In March 1896, she had a premature baby who died after only a few hours of life. José buried him on the property.

At the suggestion of a friend, José asked the governor for either a trial or his freedom. The governor gave him the freedom to go work as a doctor in Cuba. José prepared for the journey. He boarded the boat, which had a port of call in Manila and arrived a day late. This caused him to miss the sailing to Europe, and he stayed on the boat in the harbor.

Although he never left the ship, José was in the port when the Katipunan began the revolution. As a result, government officials blamed him, although José had not supported the revolution.

He felt it was too early for a revolution – that more funds and weapons were needed to achieve victory. As the revolution spread, even Filipinos who were not involved were arrested and placed in prison as suspected rebels. This included José who was arrested and charged with rebellion and sedition. The Spanish military court sentenced him to death by firing squad. While in his prison cell at Fort Santiago, José wrote the poem "Mi Ultimo Adios" (which translated means "My Last Farewell.") He had hidden the poem inside a lamp and gave it to his family. On 30 December 1896, José had confessed to a priest and then received Holy Communion. Within a chapel at the fort, José was finally allowed to marry his fiancée, Josephine. The wedding ceremony began at 5 a.m.

After they were officially married, instead of a honeymoon, they would proceed to the execution site. Josephine accompanied José who was being escorted to the Campo de Bagumbayan. While in an open field overlooking the South China Sea, José was executed by firing squad.

No Time To Lose
───────────────

The day after the execution, Josephine arrived at a camp of insurgents. She was given command of a company of soldiers. She fought for many weeks in active combat and then found that José had been correct. The Filipinos did not have enough quality weapons to obtain victory. She escaped through Japan and then headed to the United States to obtain firearms. Her friends convinced her not to return to the Philippines and the certain death, which waited if she was captured. The day of execution for José is still held in solemn memory in the Philippines with 30 December as José Rizal Day.

The Filipinos fought the Spanish for two years. Then, the United States and Spain entered into war. The Spanish were defeated, placing the Philippines under U.S. control. The Philippines underwent several changes in its legislature and government. Finally on 4 July 1946 by joint agreement, the Philippines became an independent nation.

JOSÉ RIZAL MERCADO (Philippines)

Born:	Died:	Age:
19 June 1861	30 December 1896	35

"One dies only once and, if one does not die well, a good opportunity is lost which will not come again. ... If one must die, let one die at least in his country, for his country, and in the name of his country."

~ José Rizal
(Reported in the book "Freedom's Martyr")

EDITH CAVELL

A sense of duty instilled in Edith Cavell by her parents led to a life of service and caring for others. Her parents, Reverend Fredrick and Louisa Sophia Cavell ironically named their first child Edith, meaning "happy in war." She was born in 1865 and raised in Swardeston, approximately four miles (six kilometers) south of Norwich, England.

In her family, before the evening meal, they would take a portion of their food and give it to someone else less fortunate. Edith enjoyed helping others and became extremely disciplined in her activities.

As the vicar of the local Anglican church, her father grew concerned that no Sunday school was available and worried where the money would come from to build one. Edith took it upon herself to write the bishop of Norwich about the situation. He replied that if the village could raise part of the funds, he would work toward the remainder.

Edith who loved painting, drawing and nature started the fund-raising by painting watercolors of flowers. She also did sketches and Christmas cards. One of her sisters helped, and the artwork was sold. In 1888, the Sunday school building became a reality for the village of Swardeston.

Eddy

Edith had a second cousin named Eddy Cavell who was three years older than she. Edith and Eddy frequently walked along the beach or the streets of Suffolk. They also went on picnics on top of the cliffs.

It is believed that they considered marriage. However, Eddy felt that he shouldn't marry anyone because he had a nervous disorder, which ran on his side of the family.

They would keep in touch via correspondence, and Eddy always enjoyed speaking of Edith. Neither one would ever marry.

Edith left home for a job as a governess with a French family in Brussels, Belgium. She taught their children until Edith's own father became ill with double pneumonia, leading her to return to England. At the age of 30, she decided to make a career change and go into nursing, which would allow her to be of service to more people. Her two sisters were also studying nursing. Her father made a recovery and lived to be 85.

Nursing – As A Profession

Edith trained and worked at several hospitals in England. Rules were severe against any flirting among students, nurses or doctors and would result in instant dismissal. At that time in England, nursing was not considered a respectable profession. Those who became nurses would most likely never marry.

In 1907, Edith was in her early 40s when she decided to return to Belgium. She had accepted a position to run the first nurses training school to be created in Belgium.

Devoted to the nursing profession, she wanted to show the dignity of serving others and that it was not a stigma.

In the beginning, not everyone supported the school because it wasn't Catholic, and Edith was considered a foreigner. Edith checked her emotions and remained tactful. As a result, she raised the caliber of the school and the nurses over the years.

Located outside of Brussels, the institute served as a nondenominational teaching facility to develop nursing skills. The teachings would be based on the concepts of Florence Nightingale, who is considered the founder of modern-day nursing.

Edith enjoyed the challenges of working at the institute in Belgium and had high expectations of the nurses. She took a break from work to visit her mom back in England for her mother's birthday on 6 July 1914. During that time, Edith learned that the Germans had taken control of Belgium and of the training institute. Despite the dangers, Edith felt compelled to return. World War I was starting.

The Red Cross Hospital

The German military made the British nurses return home and replaced them with German nurses. The exception was Edith who was allowed to stay and remain in charge. The facility was turned into a Red Cross Hospital, meaning persons of all nationalities could be assisted without the staff facing repercussions for giving treatment. Edith made it clear to the nursing staff that all patients would receive their best care, regardless of nationality – whether the soldier was Belgium, French, English or German. During one battle in the town of Mons located in southwest Belgium, many soldiers had been separated from their units during an Allied retreat. As a result, they were stranded behind enemy lines unable to return to their regiments.

Going Underground

With the guidance of a Belgian native, two English soldiers made it to the Red Cross Hospital, where Edith worked. One had been wounded, and the other was in good health. They asked Edith for help beyond medical treatment.

This started Edith's participation in an underground operation helping Allied soldiers escape. Soldiers were not only nursed back to health but were fed and sheltered until time for the next stop on the underground. She helped with false identification papers, even taking some of the passport photos herself. Whether she was helping a sick patient or a soldier escape, Edith was still saving lives.

When well enough to travel, each man was given 25 French francs and a guide to help make it to the neutral country of the Netherlands. Edith repeated this scenario many times over the course of a year. She worked to help from 200 to 275 soldiers of English, French and Belgium forces. After making it to neutral territory, some soldiers returned to their previous units; others returned to their native countries.

La Libre Belgique (Free Belgium)

Another key member of the underground was a Belgian architect named Philippe Baucq. He acted as a circulation manager for a resistance newspaper called La Libre Belgique. He distributed the paper via bicycle and then later on foot. Others were also involved in the production and distribution of the newspapers, which were even intentionally distributed to German officers.

Infuriated, the Germans sent special police from Berlin to find the culprits. In the summer of 1915, police were watching a suspect who went to visit Philippe Baucq. The police then entered Philippe's home and found the newspapers plus a letter from Edith Cavell.

Arrested

The German secret police was closing in on the underground operation. From 31 July through 5 August 1915, 35 persons at different points along the route were arrested. Edith was one of those persons.

The secret police often arrested persons on suspicion then investigated for evidence. Edith had been told if she cooperated they would not be as hard on the others arrested. She made a full confession.

The German military viewed her assistance to troops of different nationalities other than her own as treason. They were especially upset over the soldiers who escaped and then returned to fight.

Out of the 35 persons arrested and tried, five were sentenced to death. Of those five, only two sentences were carried out – the Belgian architect's and Edith's.

Edith received her sentence on 11 October 1915 with the execution to take place the next morning. Edith was allowed to see an English minister on her final evening. Instead of bitterness toward her captors and her fate, Edith had found great comfort in the books she was able to read again while in prison -- a Bible, her Prayer Book and "The Imitation of Christ" by Thomas À Kempis.

She used the 10 weeks while incarcerated to read, reflect and appreciate a life, which had gone by incredibly fast.

The guards came for Edith and Philippe at dawn. They were taken to the execution area – a Belgian rifle range named Tir National. They were tied to separate posts. Edith was blindfolded. After the execution, she was initially buried on site.

After her death, Edith's copy of the book "The Imitation of Christ" was given to Eddy. She had written on the inside: "With love to E.D. Cavell."

He arranged to have a special Edith Cavell edition published of "The Imitation of Christ." This version contained reproductions of her written notes and underlining.

Aftermath

When word spread by foreign ambassadors and by the press about the fate of Edith Cavell, voluntary enlistment in the English forces doubled over the succeeding eight weeks.

Buried initially in Belgium, Edith's body was exhumed after World War I ended to be relocated to her native soil. From Belgium to England, her coffin was escorted at different stages by the army, the navy and the nursing services. Her remains traveled by ocean ship, by carriage and by train, which was met by civilians at train stops along the way.

A memorial service held 15 May 1919 in Westminster Abbey was attended by the royal family of England. In the final group of pallbearers who carried the coffin was a sergeant who had been saved via the underground. He had spent the last Christmas that Edith had at the Belgium hospital.

Her final burial was at Life's Green at the Norwich Cathedral. She had finally returned to the area where she grew up – as the daughter of the village vicar.

EDITH LOUIS CAVELL (England)		
Born: 4 December 1865	Died: 12 October 1915	Age: 49

"I have seen death so often that it is not strange or fearful to me. . . . Life has always been hurried and full of difficulty. This time of rest has been a great mercy. Everyone here has been very kind." ~ Edith Cavell

(Reported in the book "Edith Cavell" by Rowland Ryder)

ROSA LUXEMBURG

Rosa Luxemburg wanted to make a difference – a difference not only for herself but for an international society. During a time when women were not part of the political process, she became a recognized speaker and writer for her views on socialism and social change.

Rosa was born in 1870 in Zamosc, in Russian-controlled Poland. She was the youngest of five children born to a working-class Jewish family. Her father inherited a timber business, which began to decline, and he moved the family to Warsaw.

At the age of five, when other children were playing and making friends, Rosa had a serious hip ailment. She became bedridden for a year and taught herself to read during that time. She was able to walk later and worked hard to minimize her limp over the years.

Swiss Education

After high school graduation, Rosa became involved in an underground socialist group, called the Proletariat at that time. To avoid arrest for her activities and to obtain a college degree, Rosa left Poland for the country of Switzerland. The University of Zürich was one of the few academic institutions allowing women in the late 1800s.

In 1889, when she left home for the new country, she also adopted a new spelling of her name. The name she was born with was Róza Luksenburg. When she registered at the university in 1980, she modified the spelling to a more cosmopolitan Rosa Luxemburg – the name she would become known by in socialist circles.

Rosa loved the beauty and peacefulness of Zürich, the capital of Switzerland. For the first time, she lived in an international community and felt more at home. Switzerland could be viewed as her own "promised land." Zürich was a refuge for those seeking diversity and more equality regardless of gender, race, religion or political focus.

In the fall of 1890, Rosa met a man who was already well known at that time for his socialist activities – Leo Jogiches. About a year later, Rosa and Leo had become lovers. However, he wanted their relationship to remain secret. They would rent rooms within walking distance of each other.

In Poland, the Proletariat political party that Rosa had belonged to no longer existed. Rosa and Leo formed a new party in 1893 called the Social Democracy of the Kingdom of Poland (SDKP).

While attending the University of Zürich, Rosa studied mathematics and natural sciences – especially botany. She then focused on economics and finally law. In 1897, she achieved a doctoral degree in law and political science. Her mother, Lina Luksenburg, died the same year.

Rosa's Family

Rosa's mother found out she had stomach cancer in April 1897. A month later, Rosa wrote her parents the news announcing that she obtained her doctoral degree.

Rosa's older sister Anna took care of their mother. She wrote to Rosa:

> "Every morning mama and papa go through prolonged negotiations about who's going to keep your letter – mama at home, just in case someone drops

by, or papa in his pocket to show it in the city."

> (Reported in the book "Rosa Luxemburg - A Life" by Elzbieta Ettinger)

Rosa never made it to see her mother that summer or fall. Her mother died on 30 September 1897. Later on, her father developed an illness. She took him on a holiday in 1899 to Silesia, Poland. She helped take care of him during the vacation. The following year, he died in 1900. Rosa was attending the Congress of the International in Paris. He had been buried for a week when she returned from the meeting.

Years later, when writing to Leo, she told of reading the letters she had received over time from her parents.

> "I read them through and cried until my eyes were swollen and went to bed wishing I'd never wake up. I cursed the damn 'politics' that stopped me from answering mother's and father's letters for weeks on end. I never had time for them."

> (Reported in the book "Rosa Luxemburg - A Life" by Elzbieta Ettinger)

The Move To Germany

In between her mother's death and her father's, Rosa would leave the country of Switzerland that she loved – for a new country – Germany. She went to Germany to further the political cause, despite the anti-Semitic environment of that country. Rosa who was Jewish entered into a marriage of convenience, which helped pave her way into Germany.

In the late 1800s, she married the son of a previous landlady. Rosa's citizenship was then classified as "Prussian," and she moved to Berlin to help cultivate German socialism. Prussia was the name of the most prominent state of Germany at that time, including the cities of Berlin, Cologne, Frankfurt and Düsseldorf.

Leo Jogiches

Leo was born in Lithuania. When he was only 21, he organized a strike of 40 workers at a printer's shop in Wilno, Lithuania. As a political agitator, he would periodically have publications or pamphlets printed and then carry out a distribution network. He had connections with smugglers and his own shop for creating passports.

In 1888, Leo spent seven days in jail. He was then released for lack of evidence. A year later, he was arrested and served four months in prison. After his release, the army inducted him into a penal battalion.

Leo's lifestyle involved secrecy. He financed his role in the cause through the money he inherited from his grandfather. His secrecy continued with his relationship with Rosa. For appearances to their friends and her family, they were only comrades. She felt that the secrecy was hypocritical.

Not only did she want others to know of their relationship, but she also wanted a child.

> "And perhaps even a baby, a very little baby?" she questioned in a letter to Leo. "Will this never be allowed?"
>
> (Reported in the book "Rosa Luxemburg - A Life" by Elzbieta Ettinger)

Rosa's marriage for citizenship ended about five years after it began on paper. She and Leo never married; nor did she ever have any children. During most of their long-term relationship, they lived in separate apartments and sometimes in separate countries.

Prison

Rosa spent much of 1902 and 1903 on speaking engagements outside of Berlin. While traveling and speaking, she co-founded a political newspaper called "Gazeta Ludowa," which is Polish for the "People's Gazette." The publication focused on working people. She handled the editorial policy, put the paper together and coordinated it from printing to distribution.

At one of her public speeches, Rosa made a comment about "a man who talks about the security and good living of the German workers has no idea of the real facts." She was referring to Emperor Wilhem II, who would be the last German Emperor and King of Prussia.

For insulting the emperor, she received three months in prison. She served a reduced sentence of six to eight weeks at the prison in Zwickau. Her shorter prison time was the result of an amnesty often offered during the coronation of a new monarch. At this time, it was King Friedrich August of Saxony.

While in prison, she caught up on correspondence and had time for reflection.

"Life constantly plays hide-and-seek with me," she wrote a friend. "It always seems to me that it is not inside me, it is not where I am, but somewhere far away."

When she was a child, she opened the window and was on the lookout for life.

"I firmly believed then that life – the real life – is somewhere far away, hidden behind tall roofs. Ever since I've been trying to find it, but it always keeps hiding behind one roof or another."

(Reported in the book "Rosa Luxemburg – A Life" by Elzbieta Ettinger)

Bloody Sunday

On 22 January 1905 in St. Petersburg, Russia, a priest led a peaceful procession of workers. They were coming to see the Russian tsar to lobby for better working conditions. The workers sang hymns and continued marching when ordered to stop. The Russian troops opened fire on the unarmed marchers.

Then, instead of singing marchers, the Palace Square was covered with hundreds of dead bodies.

This day became known as the "Bloody Sunday" massacre. This massacre resulted in a wave of strikes throughout Russia and Poland. As a result of the strikes, membership escalated in the political parties.

Leo moved to Kraków, which was in Austrian-controlled Poland. He was going to edit the political newspapers and handle pamphlets.

Rosa then went back to her native Warsaw, Poland, to write and participate in the upheaval. Twice as many workers in Warsaw were striking versus in St. Petersburg, Russia, to obtain better wages.

The Mass Strike

In Germany, there was concern that strikes would spread to this country. At a conference, the leadership of the German Trade Unions declared that mass strikes were not even to be discussed. Rosa would mock this viewpoint stating that the trade union leaders were concerned about spilling the blood of the membership. Yet, the workers themselves were prepared to sacrifice for their own interest. She would quote a publication called the "Communist Manifesto" and say:

> "We are in bloody earnest when we appeal to the masses [saying]: the workers have nothing to lose but their chains – but a whole world to gain."
>
> (Reported in the book "Rosa Luxemburg - A Life For The International" by Richard Abraham)

As a result, she earned the nickname "Bloody Rosa" or "Red Rosa." In March 1906, both Rosa and Leo were arrested. The authorities had found literature and correspondence, which were declared illegal. The prosecution was working to show that they intended to overthrow the tsarist government.

In the end, Rosa's family and friends raised enough money for a bribe to a Russian officer (approximately 2,000 rubles for him), and then another 3,000 rubles were spent on bail money.

In November 1906, Rosa did not appear at her court date. The court found Rosa and Leo guilty of belonging to the Social Democracy Party and attempting to overthrow the Russian empire. Even though Rosa had a medical certificate sent declaring she was ill, she was still declared a law evader. Three months later, a judge sentenced Leo to eight years in prison.

Costia Kautsky

Rosa offered to help some of her friends with their young adult son who seemed to have difficulty finding his path in life. She even offered to let him move in with her in the city where he would be closer to the university.

His name was Costia Kautsky. Costia moved into Rosa's flat. She returned from a trip in September 1906, and Costia had already settled in. Both Rosa and Costia enjoyed taking long walks, listening to music and reading novels. They discussed the articles she wrote. He was supportive of her writing versus Leo's previous criticisms. She provided him with the encouragement that some people find their paths later in life than others. They provided each other with the positive influence they needed. They became lovers.

Though Costia stayed with Rosa for a while, he still lived overall at his mother's home. Rosa received news that Leo escaped from the Warsaw prison in March 1907. Rosa wrote Costia to advise him of the news and the likely possibility that Leo would show up in Berlin.

When Leo arrived in early April 1907, Rosa advised him that their common-law marriage was over. He reacted violently, which frightened Rosa. He refused to move out of the apartment, and he even threatened to kill her.

Finally, Leo did move out in mid-September and headed for Finland. He had obtained a political seat. When Leo returned to Berlin in January 1908, this time he stayed in a hotel room.

When Costia returned in August 1909 from his summer vacation, he did not contact Rosa with details of his trip. She confirmed her suspicions that he was ready to end their relationship as lovers.

During the time of her relationship with Costia, Rosa received an invitation to teach at a Social Democratic Party School in Berlin. She realized that she could earn more money and have more time for economic studies by teaching rather than continuing with political journalism.

Letters From Prison

Rosa delivered a speech in 1913 (before the start of World War I), where she urged the workers of Germany not to take arms against those of other countries. She was arrested for public disobedience and placed on trial. Rosa received a one-year sentence which her lawyer, Paul Levi, appealed. During her trial, Rosa stated:

> "Wars can be conducted only if the working people see them as just and necessary, or at least accept them passively. But once the majority of the working people concludes – and it is precisely the task of Social Democracy to arouse that consciousness and lead them to this conclusion... that wars are barbaric, deeply immoral, reactionary, and against the interests of the people, then wars will become impossible."
>
> (Reported in the book "Rosa Luxemburg – A Life" by Elzbieta Ettinger)

Rosa had a love affair with her defense counsel that lasted for about six months. However, the friendship continued for the rest of her life.

At the beginning of World War I, the Social Democratic Party supported the German government, but Rosa opposed it. She and a small group of socialists formed their own party, called the Spartacus League. The Spartacus League dedicated itself to ending the war through revolution and the creation of a proletarian government, referring to government of the working class.

Because of her strong opposition to the war, Rosa was imprisoned. It's estimated she wrote hundreds of letters from prison to her friends. She encouraged others to "remain a Mensch," someone who still sees beauty in the world despite its horrors of death and destruction. While in prison, she delighted in seeing the clouds, the birds and even the weeds.

After World War I had ended, Rosa was released from prison in November 1918. She demanded political power for the working class and became frustrated by the conservative Socialist Party. The Spartacus League evolved into the German Communist Party. However, unlike standing behind an overall central committee, Rosa always promoted social democracy for individuals.

Rosa's Rallies

Rosa held rallies for the masses to bring about political debate. Her revolutionary ideas were feared by both the government and big business.

On 15 January 1919, German soldiers took Rosa and another leader of the German Communist

Party Karl Liebknecht into custody. They were brought to a hotel in Berlin.

A reward of 100,000 deutsche marks had been placed on their heads. Karl and Rosa were each taken separately from the hotel. Upon leaving, each one was knocked unconscious and placed in a waiting car.

Karl was shot, and the murderers took his body to a local mortuary. Another killer shot Rosa in the head while they were in the car. Her body was dumped in the Landwehr Canal.

The killers belonged to an illegal paramilitary organization, which would later serve as a recruiting ground for Adolf Hitler's storm troopers.

On 8 May 1919, a court martial was held for two members on an "attempted murder" charge for Rosa because her body had not been located yet.

The two men were dismissed from the service and received only a two-year sentence. However, one man was immediately released instead of going to jail because it was said he had already suffered enough. The other man served only days in prison before he was illegally released.

Those charged with Karl's murder were found "not guilty" on all charges.

Leo had most likely helped bring the court martial proceedings about by publishing a detailed article on the murders. After those charged had been set free, Leo was murdered that same month in May of 1919.

Rosa's body washed up on 31 May 1919 in the Landwehr Canal. The burial was 13 June 1919 in Friedrichsfeld Cemetery, the final resting place of other socialist revolutionaries.

The remains of Rosa Luxemburg were buried, but her spirit moved on to her next "real life."

In Tribute

In September 2006, 87 years after the murder of Rosa, the city of Berlin unveiled a monument in tribute to her. Located in what was previously the communist section of East Berlin, the monument resides in Rosa Luxemburg Platz. The monument includes quotes from her writings, which have been placed on metal strips.

One of the timeless quote's displayed for Rosa includes:

> "Ultimately all workers should receive a pension in their old age – after the 60th birthday – one that would at least

offer them the possibility of living with their families without misery."

(Reported in The Australian, www.theaustralian.news.com.au)

ROSA LUXEMBURG (Poland)		
Born: 5 March 1870	Died: 15 January 1919	Age: 48
"Freedom only for the supporters of the government, only for the members of one party – however numerous they may be – is no freedom at all. Freedom is always and exclusively freedom for the one who thinks differently." ~ Rosa Luxemburg (Reported in the book "Rosa Luxemburg" by J.P. Nettl)		

EMILIANO ZAPATA

In a small village in southern Mexico, farmers plow the fields with mules and clear the brush with machetes – at least those who are fortunate enough to have any land follow these practices. Over the past 100 years, some progress has been made with land reform in rural Mexico. The seeds of land reform came from the ideas advocated by Emiliano Zapata.

The Early Years

At the time of the birth of Emiliano Zapata, a dictator ruled Mexico in the late 1800s. The dictator had policies, which favored large wealthy plantations. Emiliano would grow up and advocate policies that favored small-farming land owners.

Emiliano's parents were mestizo, meaning their heritage was a mixture of native Indian and Spanish. Approximately, a third of the population was mestizo while Emiliano was growing up.

His parents had 10 children, but only four lived to see adulthood – Emiliano, an older brother and two sisters. They lived in a home built of stone and adobe brick. The home had a dirt floor and a thatch roof. The family raised cattle and bred horses, which would help Emiliano become an excellent horseman. Both horses and guns were part of his family's rural life.

His uncle taught him how to shoot a rifle and hunt for deer. He enjoyed listening to family stories of the battles they had fought in – especially how his ancestors fought injustice at the hand of Spanish conquistadors.

The Village

The country of Mexico comprises 31 states. Of those, one of the smaller ones is the state of Morelos. Located about 50 miles (80 kilometers) south of Mexico City, it is slightly smaller than the size of Delaware in the United States. Even though small in land size, the soil was viewed as some of the richest in the country. They lived in a village called Anenecuilco, which means the "place where the waters swirl." The history of the village goes back to the time of the Aztec Indians. It was always the place that Emiliano most wanted to be, whenever his work and his causes took him away from home.

In 1894, Emiliano's parents died within a year of each other while he was a teenager. Emiliano used his part of the inheritance to purchase 10 mules. The mules were used for transporting corn at first. Then, he started hauling bricks and lime for construction projects. He grew watermelons and was most excited one day to earn from 500 to 600 pesos when the crop was harvested.

Emiliano loved the land and the native traditions. He viewed the village almost in a spiritual way like his Indian ancestors did.

In addition to his love of the land, Emiliano was known for his love of the ladies. In his late 20s, he became involved in a scandal. He allegedly abducted a woman and set up house with her in 1908. Her mother reported Emiliano to the authorities who forced him to serve in the 7th Army Battalion. The following year, he bribed his way out of the service and back home. The woman, Inés Alfaro, stayed and had a son named Nicolás with Emiliano, plus two daughters.

Emiliano's reputation as a horseman led to an invitation to manage the stables and be a horse trainer for a rich man in Mexico City. The thoroughbred Arabian horses lived like royalty in a palace-like stable, featuring floors of marble and tiny cobblestones. Meanwhile, Emiliano saw the employees living in squalor compared to the fancy stables. After a month, Emiliano quit and decided to return home to the village.

The Village Chief

In 1909, the townspeople of Anenecuilco elected Emiliano as the village chief. One of the first tasks that he and the village secretary did was to study all of the historical documents related to the land. Most of the documents were written in the language of Nahuatl, a tribe related to the Aztecs but comprising only about 10 percent of the population at that time.

A priest was hired to translate all of the documents including title deeds, maps, legal opinions and land charters. The translated documents were placed in a tin box and buried so that others would not destroy the village's rights to the land.

The Haciendas

A hacienda refers to a large estate or ranch. In Mexico, haciendas developed a negative reputation because of the way the large plantations treated neighbors with small tracts of land.

Hacienda owners started fencing in what had been village communal land as part of their personal property. When Emiliano's or another family's livestock wandered past the moved border, the hacienda impounded the livestock. An animal would be kept without being fed until the owner came to pay a fine. Or, in the case of multiple livestock, one animal would be kept as the fine and the others returned. Emiliano tried to go through the proper channels to have the haciendas stop these practices, but it was to no avail. Finally, Emiliano advised the other farmers they could not depend on the government to return the stolen parcels of land. They needed guns and horses to reclaim their land.

In their village, the neighboring hacienda had encroached on most of the villagers' land. Emiliano organized an armed force of 80 villagers. They began occupying the disputed territory. This time, the courts started ruling in their favor.

Now, farmers started working the fields with a rifle over their shoulder. This was used to defend property and / or fight in local skirmishes as needed.

The Indians used the land to grow corn for their own food supply. But the hacienda owners wanted to grow sugar cane for export due to high prices at that time in the world marketplace. To confiscate land and to prevent farmers from reclaiming their own land, the land barons often hired former criminals to patrol the haciendas.

Debt Slaves

Problems continued with the haciendas. It was estimated by 1910, that 96 percent of the rural families did not own "any" land. Once the land was lost, some people became day laborers at the hacienda or worse yet were debt peonage. This is where someone is forced into servitude to pay off a debt.

In these cases, the workers lived on the hacienda and were forced to buy food and clothing from the hacienda store. Schoolteachers on site were forbidden to teach math so that no one could double check the figures. The debt slaves were legally bound to stay until everything was paid off. When workers died, the children entered into servitude to pay off the parents' debts.

By 1910, an estimated 60 percent of the country's Mexican population was classified as debt slaves.

The Mexican Revolution

In 1910, the Mexican Revolution started with Emiliano guiding forces in southern Mexico, and Pancho Villa overseeing rebels in northern Mexico. The rebels felt the only way to gain the attention of the Mexican government was through the use of force. Rebels were instrumental in the removal of the dictator in May 1911. He left the country to go into exile.

In June 1911, Emiliano married Josefa Espejo of Ayala in a civil ceremony. She was the daughter of a prosperous livestock dealer. Several years before, he had asked for her hand while her father was alive. He had refused because Emiliano did not own enough land.

With her father deceased and Emiliano's status as a general, the wedding could proceed. Emiliano's common-law marriage and other affairs were not considered an issue. In August of that year, they had a religious ceremony. And then, they delayed the honeymoon until the fall because the federal army attacked the state of Morelos.

Francisco Madero

In October 1911, Francisco Madero became the elected president of Mexico. Emiliano had supported President Madero during the revolution because of his pledge for land reform. However, the president started to compromise with the land owners and weakened his stance, saying he would urge the state governments to explore land reform. He also asked Emiliano to disarm his revolutionary force because Mexico was at peace in his opinion.

For a while, Emiliano's forces were voluntarily disarmed of weapons they brought in and received payment for. The haciendas continued to fence off village land. And Emiliano realized that nothing was going to change under this president.

Plan Of Ayala

In November 1911, Emiliano issued the Plan of Ayala, calling for land redistribution. Emiliano worked with a teacher named Otilio Montaño to create the dramatic reform plan.

The plan was preceded by much fanfare. In the small town named Ayala, farmers assembled who played drums and horns to perform Mexico's national anthem. Then Emiliano entered wearing the flag of Mexico like a cloak and read a document named the Plan of Ayala.

The plan advocated taking a third of the land from the haciendas and giving the land to the local councils to redistribute to the population. Pensions would be paid to those left as widows and orphans by the war. In one part, the plan stated:

> "The immense majority of Mexican pueblos and citizens are owners of no more than the land they walk on, suffering the horrors of poverty without being able to improve their social condition in any way or to dedicate themselves to industry or agriculture, because lands, timber, and water are monopolized in a few hands."
>
> (Reported in "Zapata and the Mexican Revolution")

The plan called for the farmers whose land had been seized illegally to reoccupy the land by force. The plan also called for the overthrow of Madero's government because he had not kept his promises.

The government thought the plan would not be taken seriously and even allowed a publication in Mexico City called Diario del Hogar to print it. But the plan was taken seriously. Within two months, land revolts spread through five states in Mexico.

The Zapatistas

The soldiers who followed Emiliano were known as the Zapatistas. Neither them nor Emiliano wore military uniforms. Instead, they often wore sombreros, white shirts and pants. Emiliano wore the charro clothes of a village leader – a short black jacket, boots, tight-fitting trousers with silver buttons down the side and an embroidered sombrero to top everything off.

Emiliano's devotion and respect to the land was similar to that of his ancestors. In meetings, he often listened while others debated, expressing his opinion quietly after others had finished. He gave his troops strict orders on how to act when in other villages. This included forbidding any drunken behavior, robbery or disorderly conduct. They would knock on doors and respectfully ask for food, expressing gratitude when it was provided. They would help villages reoccupy lands confiscated by the hacienda owners.

There were not enough weapons for everyone. Men who were called "buzzards" would follow the Zapatistas. They would wait until the end of a skirmish and then go out on the battlefield, taking the guns and ammunition of the dead soldiers.

When the Zapatistas captured federal soldiers, their fate depended on their rank. If they were federal officers who burned villages or executed prisoners, they would be shot. If they were regular soldiers, they gave them food and money for their weapons and return trip home. Or they could join the Zapatistas if they desired. Some did join because many of the federal soldiers were peasants who had been forced to join that army.

One of the federal prisoners who had been released was so astonished that he helped the rebels obtain guns and ammunition from federal supply depots.

When federal forces captured Zapatista rebels, they were taken to the nearest town to dig their own graves. Then they would be shot. Sometimes, when prisoners were taken from a battle, they would be hung from trees. Corpses would be left as a dangling reminder.

It cost money to operate a revolution and by May 1912, the Zapatistas were running out of funds. To help raise money, the Zapatistas started imposing a weekly tax on the haciendas and setting a minimum wage to be paid to the laborers. For those haciendas who didn't pay, the Zapatistas burned their sugar cane fields. By the beginning of 1913, it is estimated more than half of the sugar cane fields in the state were burned.

The Federal General

A general in the president's own federal army issued the order for President Madero's arrest. The fighting lasted for 10 days in Mexico City with numerous human rights abuses on the civilian population. The senior officials who were democratically elected were held as prisoners. On 22 February 1913, the president and vice president of Mexico were executed by being shot.

General Victoriano Huerta declared himself president after the coup. Those in power now were the worst enemies of the Zapatistas and would not support any land reform.

Huerta crushed the freedom of the press, which had been operating in Mexico. He closed some newspapers. Others were severely censored. His generals were appointed to take control of the state governments. Mexico became extremely militarized as the government took over the use of the railroads and the schools. Huerta increased taxes on businesses and forced companies to make loans to the government.

U.S. President Woodrow Wilson refused to recognize this Mexican government who had overthrown the leaders chosen by the people. In addition, the U.S. Government authorized the sale of arms to Pancho Villa's rebel forces in the north, which was the closest to the U.S. border.

The U.S. Government received information that a German ocean vessel was bringing a shipment of firearms and ammunition to the Huerta regime. The U.S. Navy blocked the port of Veracruz so that the delivery could not be made. The United States attacked the following day on 21 April 1914 and took the city. This resulted in the deaths of 200 Mexican soldiers, 21 U.S. service personnel and an unknown number of civilians. President Wilson was surprised when the rebels condemned the U.S. action.

However, the rebels were not interested in joining forces with Huerta to fight the U.S. As Huerta's army re-grouped to prepare against any further U.S. force, the rebels entered the towns that had been evacuated.

The Huerta regime declined, and he resigned that same year on 15 July 1914. He boarded an ocean vessel and went into exile in Cuba.

With Huerta's departure, another rebel leader General Venustiano Carranza took control of the country's capital, Mexico City. Two months later, in October 1914, revolutionary leaders and their delegates held a convention. They called for new presidential elections. Plus, they agreed to support the Plan of Ayala and use it as a basis for a future constitution.

The United States had left Mexico but remained a supporter of this convention and of Pancho Villa.

Carranza and his forces vacated Mexico City for Veracruz. Zapata and his forces then entered Mexico City on the evening of 24 November 1914. Carranza's men had vandalized and plundered the city, including the government's archives. Emiliano who couldn't stand large cities was already looking forward to returning to the village. He always enjoyed talking with the villagers in the plaza while having a brandy and cigar.

The Zapatistas stayed only a few days in Mexico City, returning home as Villa's troops entered the city to take over.

Villa And Zapata Meet

On 4 December 1914, Pancho Villa and Emiliano Zapata met for the first time. Their staffs had met before, and the leaders certainly knew of each other. The meeting took place at a school in a village about 12 miles (19 kilometers) south of Mexico City. The school had flowers and decorations for the occasion, plus a choir of children and even a mariachi band.

Otilio Montaño who worked with Emiliano on the Plan of Ayala introduced the two leaders. They had both come from rural backgrounds and both led rebel forces.

At first, it seemed awkward as to how to break the ice. They found common ground in their disapproval of Carranza. They each stated that they had no political ambitions. Pancho felt he lacked the education. His view was that the president should be an educated man, a statesman who would represent the country well to foreign dignitaries and members of congress.

Pancho expressed his support of land reform, but they did not discuss specifics. They did discuss having a combined campaign against Carranza. Pancho promised artillery and ammunition for Emiliano's forces.

After the meeting, Emiliano had to send several requests before Pancho provided the artillery. He finally came through with the artillery but not the transportation to deliver it. The handling of this combined with intelligence reports that Emiliano received made him wary and unable to trust Pancho.

Agrarian (Land) Reform

Emiliano had already started implementing the Plan of Ayala in his home state. Pensions were provided for widows and orphans of the Zapatistas. Also, lands were distributed to the villages. In January 1915, 41 surveyors came to Morelos from the National School of Agriculture. They had been sent to accurately record the boundaries of every village in the state. They would use maps and records dating back hundreds of years to establish the traditional claims.

Once a village knew the size of its land, it could keep it as communal property or divide it into individual titleholders. Each village would decide on its own, based on local customs. Part of the requirements was that no one could sell or rent the land to prevent corruption.

The Zapatistas also passed the most radical land reform bill on 26 October 1915. The legislation set a maximum size on farms, depending on the quality of the land. One farmer with good quality soil and irrigation could have up to 247 acres. While one with poor quality acreage, could have 10 times that amount with 2,471 acres. If an individual farm family left their land uncultivated for more than two consecutive years, it reverted to the state.

The Zapatistas had their own minister of agriculture. He had the authority to create agricultural banks, courts, experimental stations and irrigation services. Agriculture had the highest precedence for water rights and regulating usage.

In the fall of 1915, the state of Morelos experienced one of the best harvests ever. The farmers grew corn, chili peppers, beans and onions. The abundant supply brought food prices in line. In cities throughout Mexico, revolutions broke out with the battle cry, "Viva Zapata" (meaning "long live Zapata").

Venustiano Carranza

Venustiano Carranza and another rebel leader worked together to push back Pancho's forces to the U.S. border. Emiliano's forces withdrew from the federal district in his home state.

Due to his victories, Carranza declared himself as president of Mexico in March 1917. Emiliano felt that this had betrayed the revolution.

Although Otilio Montaño and Emiliano had collaborated on the published reform plan, they later diverged in their viewpoints. They had opposing views on which political leaders to support, and Otilio wanted them both to flee the revolutionary fight. In 1917, Otilio attempted to switch sides to the enemy territory; he was tried and then executed by a Zapatista firing squad.

During a political amnesty, Emiliano lost some of his commanders who went over to the government's side. He became depressed, wondering if the deaths and destruction had been worth the gains.

Flu Pandemic

A worldwide Spanish flu pandemic spread killing 40 million people. Of that amount, 300,000 were in Mexico. By December 1918, some cities were ghost towns. Emiliano's home state had lost a quarter of its population – some of it was attributed to death and the rest to fear as there was an exodus to a neighboring state. This state was supposedly free of the deadly virus.

The Letter

Emiliano worried about the loss of manpower and how he would defend the villages. Federal troops kept coming back to Morelos. Emiliano needed hope. He had heard of a disagreement where a federal general had ordered an officer to lead a patrol. Instead, the officer had gone to a bar where he was caught.

Emiliano wrote the officer named Colonel Jesús Guajardo and invited him and his troops to join the Zapatista side. Before the letter reached the colonel, it was intercepted by the general. The general offered the colonel the choice of a court martial followed by a firing squad or he could lure Emiliano into a government trap.

The colonel agreed to the trap and responded to Emiliano that he wanted to defect and bring his entire unit and a large supply of ammunition with him. Emiliano's generals advised that the offer seemed too good to be true. As a test of loyalty, Emiliano asked the colonel to arrest the Zapatistas who had gone to the other side. He arrested them and then proceeded to have them shot as well.

The two leaders were to meet at a railway station with 30 soldiers each. The colonel came with all 600 of his men. He advised Emiliano that he was concerned they would not remain loyal if left behind.

As a gift, he presented Emiliano with a lovely horse called the Golden Ace. They agreed to meet again the next day. On 10 April 1919, Emiliano went to the Chinameca Hacienda in Morelos for the meeting.

Emiliano obtained 150 reinforcements. The morning meeting was interrupted by reports of enemy troops nearby. Emiliano and his men left to scout the area. They returned that afternoon. Emiliano rode through the gates on the Golden Ace horse. Ten of his men escorted him. He dismounted and walked toward the steps.

The colonel's soldiers were lined up as an honor guard. A bugler played the honor call. At a designated time, the soldiers raised their guns in unison and shot Emiliano in the back.

Afterward

The following year, one of Carranza's generals Ávaro Obregón broke off and announced his intention to run for president. Obregón, the remaining Zapatistas and other revolutionaries overthrew Carranza, who was killed during this time.

The year 1920 is considered the end of this Mexican Revolution period which spanned 10 years and killed anywhere from 1 to 2 million people.

In 1920, Obregón did become president of Mexico. He was flexible and sympathetic to the cause of the Zapatistas. He began implementing many of Emiliano's reforms.

Emiliano Zapata never wavered in his principles for "Land and Liberty." Throughout the 20th century and beyond, his ideals still live in the minds of many Mexicans who want to be self-sufficient.

EMILIANO ZAPATA (Mexico)		
Born: (estimated) 8 August 1879	Died: 10 April 1919	Age: 39

"They feel so much love for the land. They still don't believe it when they're told: 'This land is yours.' They think it's a dream. But after they've seen other people drawing crops from these lands they, too, will say: 'I'm going to ask for my land and I'm going to sow there.' "

~ Emiliano Zapata

(Reported in "Villa And Zapata")

MICHAEL COLLINS

In the 12th century, Anglo-Normans invaded Ireland. England ruled the land creating laws, which discriminated against Catholics and resulted in frequent rebellions. After nearly 700 years of British oppression, the stage was being set for change – for new leaders and political organizations.

One of the future leaders was Michael Collins, born in 1890 as the youngest of eight children. His father was in his 70s and his mother was in her 30s at the time of Michael's birth. He grew up on his family's 90-acre farm called Woodfield. Michael was only six years old when his father died. However, he had already instilled in him a sense of nationalism by teaching him patriotic ballads and poems.

Michael attended a nearby school called the National School at Lisavaird. The British Government established the school with the intent to remove any Irish nationalism from the children. Ironically, one of the teachers was doing just the opposite. He belonged to the Irish Republican Brotherhood (IRB), a political group who believed in an independent Ireland, even if that meant physical force.

London, England

The post office employed thousands of persons in the United Kingdom during the early part of the 20th century. It became known as what we would call an equal opportunity employer – even for the Irish. Hiring and promotion was done based on merit. To have a position, you needed to earn good scores on the civil-service exams.

Michael excelled in school, and at the age of 15, he passed an exam for a boy clerkship, which led to a job at the London Post Office. He moved in with one of his sisters to a suburb called West Kensington. He would discuss theater and literature with his sister. He favored modern and realistic plays created by younger playwrights.

Later on, he would go to pubs for entertainment, drinking whiskey and smoking cigarettes. The use of obscenities was a second language for him, especially in certain settings.

In addition to work, entertainment and night classes, he was also involved with the Gaelic Athletic Association (GAA). This was a community inside of London dedicated to all things Irish. This meant playing Irish games, purchasing clothes and other goods made in Ireland, reading Irish literature and, if possible, speaking Gaelic, the traditional language of Ireland. The purpose was to retain the Irish culture that the English had tried to eradicate.

In his third year in London, Michael joined the Irish Republican Brotherhood. A colleague from the post office swore Michael in that November of 1909. He later obtained a position of responsibility as treasurer for several chapters of the organization.

In 1914, Michael also signed up as a member of the Irish Volunteers, a paramilitary organization, and participated in drills at King's Cross. Michael would have several different jobs while in London. In 1916, he gave his last employer there notice and said he would be leaving to fight in the war. (World War I had been going on for two years.) The employer thought Michael would be joining the British forces and gave him a bonus before leaving. But Michael would be joining the Irish forces to fight against the British in a different war.

Easter Rising

Back in Ireland, Michael would not be working in the post office but helping to take it over. At noon on Easter Monday, 24 April 1916, members of both the Irish Volunteers and the Irish Republican Brotherhood rebelled against British authority. Michael, who was 26, assisted a group who took control of the General Post Office in Dublin.

The rising lasted for almost a week. It was put to an end by British troops. At first, the general Irish population did not support the insurgency because some had family in the British army fighting World War I in France.

However, Irish public sentiment changed in the aftermath of the rising. The British Army arrived in the evening of the same day that the rising started. Two groups of reinforcements came the next day. One group arrived on a gunboat and bombarded the street the post office was on, killing and injuring hundreds of civilians. British soldiers captured Irish rebel leaders and executed 16 men. One rebel leader could not stand, so he was strapped to a chair and shot. An estimated 1,800 persons, including Michael, were placed in British prison camps.

Prison Camps

Michael went with a group of prisoners sent on a cattle boat the evening of 1 May 1916. He was part of the group taken to Stafford Detention Barracks in Wales. After a few months, they were transferred to Frongoch in the northern Welsh countryside.

The Irish prisoners were being brought together from the different prison camps for processing. Those with minor charges were let go. The most troublesome rebels would be re-assigned to a prison. Those in the middle would stay at Frongoch, which was the site of an abandoned whisky distillery.

Michael remained at Frongoch Prison Camp, which the Irish referred to as Sinn Féin (pronounced "shin fane") University because it helped re-invigorate the political revolutionary movement. Friendships became stronger and so did the call for solidarity.

In the meantime, the British authority grew concerned about the American government who condemned the action. The U.S. government was sensitive to the many Americans of Irish descent. Because of American pressure, the British released the Irish prisoners in less than a year – just a few days before Christmas.

After returning to Ireland, Michael found work as a secretary at the Irish National Aid and Volunteer Dependants Fund. Michael's leadership skills had started developing more while in prison, where he had helped publicize the grievances of the inmates. This actually helped him obtain his new position.

The national aid fund helped those affected by "the rising." Michael was deeply concerned by those still spending their lives in prison. He sent them food, letters, books, publications and money. He helped arrange visitors. And most important, when a prisoner was released, he made sure the person was taken care of with a place to stay and the transport home to Ireland.

In January 1919, the Sinn Féin organization announced that instead of participating in the British Parliament in London, it would establish its own government. Called Dáil Éireann, it signified an independent Irish Parliament. The membership elected Eamon de Valero as president and Michael as minister of finance.

In his role for the Irish Volunteers, Michael served as director of organization, intelligence and communications.

Spies And Assassins

In Michael's analysis of the failure of the previous rising – a main contributor was espionage. Spies infiltrate revolutionary organizations or overhear talk at a pub, and the information is reported to the British spy network. At that time, it was located in Dublin Castle.

The British spies were also referred to as 'G' men. Near the end of a shift, each G-man would transfer reports into a huge ledger that all members of the division could access at the Great Brunswick Police Station. The information would be analyzed, and the most important information sent to Dublin Castle.

Michael had some spies who volunteered their services out of nationalistic pride. Others, he would recruit. Some of them already worked in Dublin Castle.

One spy who volunteered her services was his own cousin. She was requested by her employer to decode messages between London – where she was based – and Dublin Castle. She would transcribe extra copies of messages while she was in the bathroom and then smuggle them out.

Michael's intelligentsia informed him that Britain was planning a major arrest of numerous Sinn Féin members. Word spread to as many as possible to avoid going home the night of the raids. Despite this effort, 80 persons were still arrested and sent to English prisons.

Late in 1920, the British established a unit referred to as the Igoe Gang. Igoe was a fictitious name, and all of the identities (of these 15 police officers) were protected. Many of them were Irish. Their role was to identify members of the Irish Republican Army who would either be arrested and tortured – or assassinated on site.

While the Igoe Gang searched for Michael and other members of the Irish Republican Army, he used his own men to counter. Michael's team of assassins was known as the "Twelve Apostles." They worked in tandem with the Dublin Brigade. In groups of two or threes, they would identify an Igoe Gang member with the touch of the nose or lifting a hat. The Apostles would shoot and kill the person and then blend into the crowd of shoppers along busy streets. The Twelve Apostles had other occupations to help provide alibis during assassinations. For example, one worked as a printer and another as a cabinetmaker.

Michael knew the British were intensifying their efforts to assassinate him. He also knew the Irish could not defeat the British forces in a full battle. However, he could wreck havoc with the British spy network.

Bloody Sunday

After the Easter Rising, support grew for organizations like Sinn Féin and the Irish Volunteers. The volunteers began re-organizing and changed its name to the Irish Republican Army (IRA) in 1918. To deal with the IRA, England sent in a special force referred to as the Black and Tans because the uniforms were similar to the coloring of a pack of hounds. The special force gained a reputation for being vicious, and atrocities took place on both sides.

When the Black and Tans went to a village where the local police station had been burned, they simply chose a house in the neighborhood and took it over. When military personnel were attacked, the British Black and Tans burned villages and their occupants or stabbed the Irish on the streets.

Michael ordered his spy network to find out the names and home addresses of another British assassin team known as the Cairo Gang. The British officers were identified and the target date was Sunday, 21 November 1920. The officers were more likely to be at home on a Sunday. The individual residences did not have security precautions because none of the spies had ever been killed at home.

Michael's Apostles spread out to the targeted residences with handguns and in some cases hatchets to break inside. The synchronized plot began at 9 a.m. Michael's assassins rang doorbells or knocked. After entering, the assassinations began. The targets were the officers. In some cases, wives or girlfriends were pulled aside while the British spies were murdered.

The Apostles killed from 12 to 14 persons during the attacks. Those who were at Dublin Castle were in shock and in panic as reports came in. News spread and hundreds of civil servants and military staff sought refuge in the castle afraid they were next on the list.

That same day, the British Black and Tans sought retribution. In the afternoon, they arrived at Dublin's Croke Park. During a football (soccer) match, they indiscriminately shot and killed 12 persons. This included one player and 11 fans. An estimated 70 persons were injured during the shooting and stampede to evacuate.

After the killings that took place by the Irish, Michael said:

> "For myself, my conscience is clear. There is no crime in detecting and destroying in wartime the spy and the informer. They have destroyed without trial. I have paid them back in their own coin."
>
> (Reported in "The Illustrated Life of Michael Collins")

Nearly six months later, Michael's home where he grew up was burned to the ground. Michael's brother, Johnny, lived in the home with his eight children. As a widower, Johnny had the housekeeper staying with the children at the time while he was attending a meeting.

British soldiers gathered up the neighbors at bayonet point and told them to place straw around the home and then throw gasoline (petrol) onto the straw. They were forced to light the fire so that the soldiers could say the Collins' own neighbors burned the home. All of the family got out of the house, but they were upset they could not save some of the possessions, such as a wooden cradle made by Michael's father.

Fires started increasing on both sides. The Irish Republican Army began burning the mansions of Irish landlords. Ireland still retains the ruins of many castles, which were burned during this time. Finally, Irish landlords convinced members of the British Parliament to stop the burning of homes and shops of Irish Republican Army (IRA) members. The fires then subsided on each side.

Katherine (Kitty) Brigid Kiernan

Kitty Kiernan and Michael met in 1917. He was originally infatuated with her sister Helen. However, Helen was already engaged to a local lawyer, and Michael could not change her mind.

Helen and Kitty along with their other siblings operated a family hotel, called the Greville Arms. It was located in the town of Granard, which is in the center of Ireland. In addition to the hotel business, the Kiernan family operated the grocery, lumber and hardware stores, plus a bar and a funeral home.

Kitty was originally dating one of Michael's close friends and colleagues. Over time, Michael persuaded Kitty to give him a chance. This was most likely during the time when his friend, Harry Boland, had gone to work in the United States for much of 1919 through 1921.

Because Michael and Kitty lived in different cities, much of their relationship occurred through occasional visits and mostly letters or notes.

Later on, Michael proposed marriage to Kitty, and she accepted, so they were officially engaged.

He would try to write her everyday, even if it was only a short note, during and after negotiations with the British to work out a peace treaty. Afterward, he wrote her on 9 February 1922, the following:

> "It was a good job you did not ask me if I enjoyed my time in London. It was heartbreaking simply – fighting the English there."
>
> (From the book "In Great Haste")

This time though, the fighting did not take place in a post office or the city streets, instead it was negotiations around a conference table.

Negotiating A Treaty

Michael continued to lose colleagues in clashes and had differences in opinions with other political leaders. He became one of the persons chosen to be on the Irish delegation headed by Arthur Griffith for peace talks in London. Negotiations started in October 1921 and were held periodically through 6 December 1921. Michael felt that Ireland's negotiating team, including himself, was inexperienced compared to the British team of Winston Churchill, Prime Minister David Lloyd George and Attorney Lord Birkenhead. Ireland's President Eamon de Valera argued that he should remain in Ireland as president during this crisis and sent the Irish delegation in his place.

Negotiations began at 10 Downing Street in London, office of the prime minister of the United Kingdom. Some of the negotiators on the English team did not want to shake the hand of Michael Collins. So the British prime minister met the Irish team at the door to usher them to their chairs and avoid handshakes. Before the negotiations each day, Michael went to Mass so that he could light a candle for Kitty.

During the negotiations, the British controlled not only the location but the agenda on the talks. As a result of the negotiations, the treaty called for an Irish Free State, and it required an oath to the King of Great Britain, which Michael had slightly modified to make it more acceptable. Ireland would be given control over its own security and over international trade, allowing it to restrict trade, even British imports, if desired.

The issue of the counties in Northern Ireland, whether they would be part of one Ireland governed from Dublin or remain under British rule, would be determined by the existing Northern Ireland Prime Minister James Craig. Later, he opted to keep the status quo and remain under British rule.

Before the issue could be sent to James Craig, the British wanted a commitment from all of the Irish delegates to support the treaty. Prime Minister George issued an ultimatum to sign now for peace or face a war within three days.

Prime Minister George needed an answer that evening, so he could advise James Craig if the talks had failed or if he would be sending approved articles of agreement. In the early morning hours of 6 December 1921, both sides signed two copies of the Anglo-Irish Treaty. After that, they all shook hands for the first time.

Those who supported the treaty included some of the younger members of the Irish Republican Army, trade unions, the church and large corporations. Those opposed to the treaty included the president of Ireland, who did not want to be part of the negotiation team, and Michael's older comrades of the Irish Republican Army.

The Anglo-Irish Treaty narrowly passed Ireland's parliament on 7 January 1922 with a vote of 64 to 57. Eamon de Valera resigned his presidency, and Arthur Griffith took his place in a transitional government. Michael was elected as chairman.

One result of the treaty was the evacuation of Dublin Castle in mid-January 1922. What remained of the British spy network went home as well as the civil servants.

In February 1922, Michael had several meetings with James Craig on Northern Ireland. After meeting in Dublin, they had several more meetings with Churchill in London. No progress was made.

The Irish Civil War started in June 1922 and would last nearly 11 months. In Northern Ireland, the Catholic population received the brunt of the attacks. Catholics were killed, homes were torched and thousands driven from their jobs.

Michael began a new role as commander-in-chief of the Free State Army. Two months after the outbreak of civil war, he left Dublin to meet with forces in the field.

Kitty had selected as their wedding date 22 August 1922. However, Michael had postponed it because he had a critical mission designed to open peace talks with the opposition.

Now instead on 22 August 1922, his convoy traveled in the south, in an area known as West Cork. Michael's convoy was attacked in an ambush by anti-treaty Irish Republican Army forces, also referred to as "irregulars." Instead of trying to drive past the barricade, Michael wanted to fight the enemy. The skirmish lasted about 30 minutes. A fellow Irishman shot Michael in the head.

Instead of a wedding date, Michael Collins had a death date. News spread quickly about the death of Michael Collins with a profound sense of loss and tragedy. Even in a prison in Kilmainham, the news that Michael Collins had been assassinated resulted in a heavy silence throughout the prison cells. Then, approximately 1,000 prisoners dropped to their knees saying the rosary out loud for the soul of Michael Collins.

His body lay in state in the Dublin City Hall, which was also the headquarters of the Irish Provisional Government. It was the building next to Dublin Castle. Paying their last respects were Irish civilians and soldiers, foreign dignitaries and even British soldiers, wearing black armbands on their uniforms.

More than 10,000 people on 28 August 1922 lined the funeral route from Dublin City Hall to the national cemetery for Irish patriots known as Glasnevin.

The coffin draped with the flag of Ireland was mounted on a gun carriage and pulled by a team of black horses. Military cars draped with black crepe and wreaths of flowers were driven behind the carriage. Adorning the flag-draped coffin was a single flower – a white peace lily – from his own Kitty Kiernan.

MICHAEL COLLINS (Ireland)

Born: 16 October 1890	Died: 22 August 1922	Age: 31

"Capitalism has come, not only to serve Britain's purpose by keeping the people divided but, by setting worker against worker, it has profited by exploiting both. It works on religious prejudices. . . . Such a policy – the policy of divide and rule, and the opportunity it gives for private economic oppression – could bring nothing but evil and hardship to the whole of Ireland."

~ Michael Collins
(Reported in the book
"Mick – The Real Michael Collins")

ENGELBERT DOLLFUSS

Physical size is not an indication of the inner strength and courage a person can possess. This was true of Engelbert Dollfuss of Austria who never grew taller than 4 feet 11 inches (1.5 meters), yet he achieved a large stature in life.

Engelbert's last name of Dollfuss came from his mother who was unmarried and was the daughter of a farmer at the time of his birth in 1892. A year later, Josepha Dollfuss would marry a farmer named Leopold Schmutz from the village of Kirnberg in Lower Austria.

Engelbert grew up on the farm and developed a deep interest in the church. He was only 12 when he expressed his desire to become a priest. He attended an Episcopal seminary and graduated in 1913. Then, at the age of 21, he became a student at the University of Vienna, where he decided to pursue law instead of religion.

The Military

World War I broke out in 1914, and Engelbert left his studies. Due to his physical size, it took two tries before he was accepted by the draft board. Engelbert joined the Imperial Army and was stationed on the Alpine front. This is where the Austrian Army and Germans fought the Italians.

In 1918, the Austro-Hungarian monarchy collapsed. Engelbert, who had risen to the rank of first lieutenant was on a three-day leave when his regiment was captured and taken to a prisoner-of-war camp.

World War I ended that same year. Austria like many countries was in political and economic distress. With the break up of the empire, Austria was left at only one-eighth of its former size.

Engelbert returned to college, where he helped pay his way by working at a farmers' union. While studying law at a university in Berlin, he met a German woman who he married in 1921.

Economic Woes

After the war, some countries refused to sell staples and food to Austria; in the capital of Vienna, citizens were facing famine conditions. In 1929, the U.S. stock market crashed, and a worldwide depression followed. Austrian citizens began to lose their jobs. Those unemployed were estimated from 300,000 to 400,000. The desperate economic outlook led to fragmented and extreme political situations.

The right wing bloc became interested in pursuing a regime similar to Italian fascism. Instead of having various political parties, fascism promotes having different classes of individuals. Groups are represented by classes of capitalists and land owners, professionals, farmers and laborers. A fascist government is led by an authoritarian leader who personifies the nation's highest values and ideals.

In terms of politics, Engelbert became active in the Christian Social Party (today it is known as the Austrian People's Party). The Christian Social Party was a conservative group, who originally worked to help the underprivileged.

During the serious financial and political troubles of Austria, Engelbert was named chancellor (prime minister) of the Austrian republic in May 1932.

At 39 years of age, he was the youngest head of government in Europe at that time.

The political times remained uncertain. Engelbert felt he could not trust his allies. On 3 October 1933, a former soldier who was mentally unstable shot at Engelbert. Although he was only slightly wounded, he had ongoing hearing loss.

Due to Austria's reduced physical size and economic woes, Engelbert wanted to ally with another country he could depend on for support. Larger, western European countries did not seem that interested in Austria at that time. Engelbert aligned himself with Benito Mussolini, the fascist dictator of Italy for advice and support. Mussolini urged Engelbert to suppress the party known as the social democrats.

The Nazi Party

In January 1933, Adolf Hitler took over as chancellor of Germany. This caused serious problems for Austria. During that same year, the Nazis began a terrorist campaign of bombings to destroy Austria's tourist trade. When the Nazis threw hand grenades at a group of auxiliary police, Engelbert decided to outlaw the party.

More than 1,100 Nazis were arrested including mayors of towns and civil servants. Some of the leaders fled to Germany where they could advocate Nazi propaganda. They even had Nazi leaflets dropped by plane into the Austrian cities of Innsbruck and Salzburg. Radio broadcasts from Munich featured pro-Nazi speeches within Austria, speaking out against Engelbert.

Those who supported Engelbert were neither Nazis nor socialists. They were mostly comprised of farmers and middle-class citizens with strong Catholic ties, those of Jewish faith and those of nobility who had been part of the former monarchy.

The Austrian Government feared the Nazi propaganda campaign would lead to more Nazis being elected to parliament.

The Heimwehr (Home Defense)

After World War I, the Imperial Army disbanded but set up volunteer defense units in rural areas and in cities. These units were known as the Heimwehr or Home Defense. The groups were mostly fascist in nature.

Engelbert's concept was to create a fascist state, which had the full backing of the Catholic

Church. Through a technicality, Engelbert was able to legally dissolve the Austrian Parliament. Then, he began to name himself to multiple cabinet positions, including:

- Minister of agriculture
- Minister of defense
- Minister of foreign affairs
- Minister of public security

With democracy suspended, Engelbert formed an organization called the Fatherland Front. He tried to appeal to Austrian pride and patriotism. A rally was held which showed the support of the Heimwehr members, the Austrian Army and the Boy Scouts. Although Austria was no longer a democracy, many felt extreme measures were needed to keep the Nazis from taking control. Engelbert became known as "Europe's most popular dictator."

Social Democrats And The Schutzbund

In Engelbert's view, the social democrats were more like communists rather than the socialists associated with the British Labour Party. This political party had its own paramilitary force, known as the Schutzbund.

Engelbert outlawed the paramilitary force and had the police conduct searches for the group's weapons.

The police raids brought bitter confrontations. Engelbert banned the Social Democratic Party itself in February 1934, which led to a brief and bloody civil war. The social democrats responded with a strike. However, before the announcements could be printed to notify everyone to go on strike, the electrical workers struck early. This pulled the electricity on the printing presses, which were suppose to announce the strike.

Engelbert's negotiations and ultimatums were not influencing the civil war. The government forces had no tear gas to control crowds because the peace treaty after World War I forbade Austria to have any chemical weapons. As an extreme alternative, the chancellor approved the army using artillery and cannons. Hundreds were killed. The war quickly ended, and the government hanged the leaders after a quick court martial. Those killed belonging to the Schutzbund were buried in a mass grave with no burial services. In contrast, those killed for the Austrian Government received flag-draped coffins and funeral services celebrating Mass.

Those who lived through it became bitter toward Engelbert and considered him the enemy, just as the Nazis did.

Operation Summer Festival

The Austrian Nazi Party included a small military unit called the Schutzstaffel (also known as the SS Standarte 89). This was a group formed from soldiers expelled from the armed forces.

The Austrian SS conspired a plot based on three strikes:

- The entire cabinet including Engelbert as prime minister would be placed under arrest.
- The president of Austria would also be captured.
- The broadcasting station in the capital, which was controlled by the federal government, would be overtaken.

The plan was to broadcast that the current government had resigned, and a new chancellor would be announced.

The plot did not go according to plan. Eight of the 10 ministers of the cabinet had already left the chancellor. Engelbert remained with two of his ministers and his assistant.

At 12:50 p.m. 25 July 1934, eight trucks of soldiers entered the courtyard, which housed the seat of the Austrian Government. This was the normal time that the crew of guards would change shifts.

Although dressed as Austrian guards, they were actually Nazis ready to stage a government coup. They disarmed the real guards. Two of the Nazis who made it inside the building found Engelbert and three of his staff members.

One of the attackers approached Engelbert who raised his hands to shield his face. According to Engelbert's personal attendant, the gunman fired twice at Engelbert from a close range. Engelbert collapsed on the floor and became unconscious.

It is believed that one of the bullets went through his spinal column causing paralysis.

Around the same time, another task force of the Nazis' special forces failed to capture the Austrian president.

Regarding the third part of the plan, others were broadcasting over the radio the bogus news that Engelbert as chancellor had resigned, and one of the Nazis was the new government leader. This did not happen because there was a Heimwehr regiment and police forces protecting the remaining cabinet members who were free.

Engelbert regained consciousness and requested to see a priest, but this was denied. He died without receiving the last rites.

While on trial for the shooting, one of the accused said he only fired one shot in self-defense. The two defendants were found guilty. They were sentenced to death by hanging.

Even though they would not obtain a priest for Engelbert, one of them gave confession to a Catholic priest – the other one received sacrament from a Protestant minister.

Their executions occurred three hours after the sentence was announced on 31 July 1934 – six days after the chancellor's death.

More death sentences and executions were later carried out related to the assassination and attempted coup. Plus, other members received prison sentences.

Engelbert was originally buried in a cemetery in Hietzing and then later moved to the Chancellors' Church in Austria. A memorial to him was created at the Church of the Dormition in Jerusalem.

Engelbert's death led to an increase in participation in the Fatherland Front, which he had created. But from now on, the Fatherland Front would be without its founding father.

ENGELBERT DOLLFUSS (Austria)		
Born: 4 October 1892	Died: 25 July 1934	Age: 41

"Authority means the orderly exercise of power – leadership by responsible and unselfish men who are prepared to sacrifice their own interests."

~ Engelbert Dollfuss
(Reported in the book
"Assassination In Vienna")

SOPHIE SCHOLL

After World War I ended in 1918, Germany strived to recover from its defeat. The following year, Adolf Hitler co-founded the National Socialist Workers' Party, which came to be known as the Nazi Party. Initially, he promised to restore Germany and bring the country back to greatness. Instead, he brought a regime filled with hatred, with mind control and with distrust. Despite his vast resources, he was not able to control everyone. One shining example is Sophie Scholl.

Sophie was born in Baden-Wurttemberg to a bourgeois (middle-class) family. She was the fourth of five children. When Sophie was seven, the family moved to Forchtenberg, where her father served as mayor. The family later moved two more times. Then at the age of 12, she and her classmates joined an organization called Hitler Youth.

The concepts of Hitler Youth conflicted with her own views as a Christian and with the political opinions of her father, friends and some teachers. To help escape the National Socialism, she read books on theology and philosophy. She used her talents to draw and to paint. She wrote essays about nature and her homeland. She dreamed of studying biology one day at a university.

Nazi Control

Life in Germany was under a complete dictatorship with the Nazi Party controlling everything from the legal system to the newspapers and the radio stations in the country. If you were caught listening to a radio broadcast from Britain, you would be executed. In addition to the media, the Nazis controlled virtually every aspect of life: all levels of education (kindergarten through college), all religious and cultural institutions, travel, all firearms, the police and the military.

Mind control started at an early age in school. Anyone could be a government informant. Children were taught to turn in their own parents if anything negative, even a joke, was made about Hitler or Nazi ideology. Every city block had a Nazi collaborator who was responsible for monitoring, documenting activities and reporting conversations of each person in that area.

With the Nazi control of education, no one could be admitted to a university without have participated in the National Labor Service. After high school, Sophie worked as a kindergarten teacher hoping this would serve as an alternative. It did not suffice, and she was chosen for six months of auxiliary war service as a nursery teacher in Blumberg, Germany.

In a letter to her brother Hans, Sophie wrote the following while at the Krauchenwies Camp near Sigmaringen, Germany, located on the Danube River. The letter, dated 2 August 1941 is published in the book "At The Heart Of The White Rose." It reads:

> "I'm still reeling under the impact of the latest, appalling piece of news: We're to do another six months compulsory war work in camps...which intends to organize our leisure time as well."

The White Rose

Finally, before her 21st birthday, she was allowed to enroll at the University of Munich, where she would study biology and philosophy. This opportunity enabled Sophie to meet philosophers, artists and writers who became important contacts to her. As part of her Christian faith, she wanted to answer the question of how an individual should act while living under a dictatorship regime.

While at the university, Sophie learned of some activities her brother was involved in. He and some of his fellow medical students had started a resistance group, which went by the name – The White Rose. Her brother, Hans, and other members were anonymously writing pamphlets and distributing them opposing the Nazi regime.

Because of the inherent dangers, Hans did not want Sophie to participate but finally relented. The small group of students were primarily Christians who had seen their Jewish friends suffer at the hands of the Nazis.

For their own protection, members of The White Rose did not tell their families about being part of the organization. Pamphlets were copied on a duplicating machine. Obtaining paper and stamps had to be done with discretion so that suspicion was not aroused. Some leaflets were mailed; others were placed in phone booths and some outside lecture halls.

The first few pamphlets called for passive resistance against the Nazis. Then, active resistance became the topic – advocating the sabotage of armament plants, obstructing research for the war effort and boycotting institutions, which enhanced the Nazi image.

Several members of The White Rose included male medical students forced to serve a three-month stint on the Russian front during 1942. They saw first hand the horror of war and the unbelievable cruelty the Nazis displayed to the Jewish population.

The White Rose produced leaflets describing the mass extermination of the Jews and of the Polish nobility. After the capture of Poland, the Nazis murdered 300,000 Jews.

Leaflets Of The Resistance

In addition to The White Rose name, the organization also used the title "Leaflets of the Resistance" for the last two pamphlets. The sixth and final pamphlet was written by Kurt Huber, a professor at the University of Munich, which stated in one part:

"We have grown up under a government which deprived us ruthlessly of free speech. Hitler Youth, SA, SS have done their utmost to force us into uniforms, revolutionize and anesthetize us during the most promising years of our lives, normally devoted to acquiring education. 'Ideological training' they termed this despicable method of stifling in a fog of empty phrases, our budding ability to think and judge for ourselves. Demonic and narrow minded at once, they train future party bigwigs in 'castles of the knightly order' to become godless, insolent and unscrupulous exploiters and murderers, to blindly and stupidly follow their Führer. They think us intellectuals appropriate stooges to fashion bludgeons for them so that they may rule."

(Reported in The History Place™, www.historyplace.com, by a survivor of the resistance group The White Rose)

On 18 February 1943, Sophie and Hans distributed the leaflets on the University of Munich campus, leaving them on window sills and outside of lecture halls while classes were in session. As they were about to leave, they tossed the remaining leaflets from a stairwell into the university courtyard. They were spotted by a janitor who held them until the Gestapo arrived.

The People's Court?

Four days after their arrest, another member of The White Rose, Christoph Probst, was also picked up. The trial began at the People's Court. Inappropriately named, the People's Court was not part of the German Constitution. Instead, it was created by the National Socialist Party to eliminate the enemies of Hitler. When Sophie arrived in court, her leg had already been broken by the Gestapo during interrogations. The presiding judge acted as if he were the prosecutor, instead of the judge. He could not understand what had happened to these young adults who came from good German families and had been members of Hitler Youth.

Because the three defendants admitted everything, no witnesses were called. The judge found all of them guilty of treason and sentenced them to death by guillotine at Stadelheim Prison in Munich. Sophie and Hans were able to see their parents one last time before the executions were carried out the same day as the trial. They each put on a brave face for their parents.

As leaders of a resistance, their earthly lives ended that day. However, they serve as a reminder that not everyone who was German was also a Nazi.

SOPHIE SCHOLL (Germany)		
Born: 9 May 1921	Died: 22 February 1943	Age: 21
"It isn't easy to banish all thoughts of the war. Although I don't know much about politics and have no ambition to do so, I do have some idea of right and wrong, because that has nothing to do with politics and nationality. And I could weep at how mean people are, in high-level politics as well, and how they betray their fellow creatures, perhaps for the sake of personal advantage." ~ Sophie Scholl's letter to a friend ("At The Heart Of The White Rose")		

RAOUL WALLENBERG

He is described as an angel of rescue. He has been credited with saving anywhere from 20,000 to more than 100,000 Jewish lives during World War II.

For the angel who rescued so many, his particular fate remains unclear. And the "true" end to this story is still not known. But here is how it all began....

Raoul Gustav Wallenberg was born in 1912 to a wealthy and prestigious family in Sweden. He was named after his father, Raoul Oscar Wallenberg, a naval officer who died of cancer before his son's birth. He was also named after his paternal grandfather, Gustav Wallenberg, a proponent of international trade and diplomacy.

Raoul's grandfather developed an ocean shipping company called East Asiatic Steamship Line. He promoted Sweden's export trade to the Far East and became the country's first envoy to Tokyo.

His mother re-married when Raoul was about five to six years old, and he would later have a stepbrother and a stepsister. While growing up, he became interested in planes and ships, including World War I battleships.

He also developed a great passion for architecture. Even as a child, Raoul wanted to visit construction sites of new developments.

In 1920, his grandfather was named Swedish minister to Turkey. He relocated to Constantinople (now known as Istanbul). Three years later, Raoul at approximately 11 years of age would travel by himself on the train to visit his grandfather in this new democracy.

While traveling, Raoul had with him a passport, which is a document identifying citizenship and enables the holder to enter into other countries. Raoul would realize later the significance of such a life-saving document.

A Global Education

His grandfather who served as a guiding force in his life emphasized the importance of knowing about other countries and about languages. Raoul became fluent in German, French and English. He even studied Russian because he thought it would be of value to him someday.

After his military service finished, his grandfather paid for him to go to the United States as a foreign exchange student. In 1931, he enrolled at the University of Michigan to study architecture. Raoul demonstrated gifted abilities as a student. During one period, he broke his right arm and had to start drawing with his left hand. He was still described as drawing better than most of the other students, even when using his left hand.

He graduated with the highest scholastic standing, and as a result, received the silver medal from the American Institute of Architects in 1935.

After college, his grandfather wanted Raoul to obtain some business experience. He arranged an unpaid six-month internship for him at an export / import trading company in South Africa. From Cape Town, Raoul wrote his grandfather about a girl he knew when he was in the United States.

"I've been rather upset the last few months, including when I was in Stockholm. A girl whom I used to spend all my time with in the United States and whom I liked very much unfortunately fell in love with me, and I've had a very difficult time of it, when everything I wrote or did only hurt her. I have found it depressing to be the cause of so much pain."

(Published in "Letters And Dispatches 1924-1944 Raoul Wallenberg")

After South Africa, his next internship was arranged at a bank in Haifa, Palestine (now known as Israel). Even though he was considered a gentile and a Christian, Raoul did have Jewish ancestry. His grandmother's grandfather was a German Jew who moved in 1780 to Stockholm, Sweden. Even back then, Germany already suffered from anti-Semitism, meaning that Jewish people were discriminated against. In 1936, Raoul met Jewish refugees from Germany. He learned that anti-Semitism still continued and was growing at an alarming rate as the Nazis created discriminatory laws.

In September 1935, Germany implemented Anti-Jewish Nuremberg Laws. This meant that Jewish individuals were no longer considered citizens of Germany. They had already been prohibited from entering any branch of the German military. Marriage and sexual relations were illegal between a German and a person of Jewish blood.

While in Haifa, Raoul's letters to his grandfather referenced the plight of the Jewish people.

> "To them, Palestine is much more than a mere refuge; it is the Promised Land, the land designated for them by God. It will take an enormous effort to make the country suitable for farming, for there is very little water and much too much stone."
>
> (Reported in the book "A Quiet Courage" by Elizabeth R. Skoglund)

On 12 March 1936, Raoul wrote his grandfather the following:

> "Poor people, they evidently have to adjust to being in a minority wherever they go. They have boundless enthusiasm and idealism and these

immediately strike you as the most common characteristics of Zionism."

(Published in "Letters And Dispatches 1924-1944 Raoul Wallenberg")

In March 1937, his grandfather died. Raoul is now on his own for finding his career path. He tried several business ventures to sell new products, but they weren't successful.

World War II

On 1 September 1939, World War II began as the Nazis invaded Poland. Two days later, both France and Great Britain declared war on Germany because of the invasion of Poland. As the Nazis entered various countries, they forced the Jewish population to identify themselves with an armband or yellow star on their clothing bearing the word "Jude," which means Jew in German. The Jewish population is excluded from all aspects of the economy and forced to live in ghettos.

In December 1941, Japan bombed a U.S. base in Hawaii called Pearl Harbor. The United States entered World War II joining the Allied forces of Great Britain, France and the Soviet Union. Fighting the Allies were the Axis powers comprising Germany, Japan and Italy.

The Scarlet Pimpernel

Raoul's half sister, Nina Lagergren, said that he had always been a fan of acting and of the movies. In the winter of 1942, they saw a movie called "Pimpernel Smith." This American film showed an absent-minded professor who saved Jewish people from Nazi oppressors. The movie was a World War II version of a classic film called "The Scarlet Pimpernel," based on a hero who uses inventive ruses to save aristocrats during the French Revolution.

Raoul and Nina enjoyed the World War II version of the "Pimpernel" movie. He told her that he wanted to do something meaningful with his life, like helping the Jewish people.

Raoul met a Hungarian Jew named Koloman Lauer, who ran an import / export business, specializing in food and delicacies. He was looking for someone to run the international division, and Raoul seemed perfect. As a citizen of a neutral country like Sweden, Raoul was still able to travel through Nazi-occupied Europe while conducting international trade.

War Refugee Board

In January 1944, U.S. President Franklin Delano Roosevelt created the War Refugee Board. The main purpose of the organization was to save Jews from Nazi persecution. The Nazis had already killed so many Jews during the Holocaust that Budapest, Hungary, was the last Jewish community left in Europe.

The representative of the War Refugee Board in Sweden assembled a committee for advice and to determine whom to send to the Swedish Legation in Budapest. Raoul's business partner, Koloman Lauer, was on the committee. He suggested that Raoul go to lead the rescue mission. Raoul had already volunteered to Koloman that he would go help the family of Koloman's wife. They were still in Hungary. After much debate, the group finally agreed on Raoul, although he was considered young at only 32 years of age. Raoul would be going with U.S. funds for the relief effort. He had obtained permission from the Swedish officials that the funds could be used for bribery if needed to save lives. He was free to establish contact with the enemy. And he could provide asylum in Swedish Legation buildings to offer protection to those in need.

Adolf Eichmann

Nearly four months before Raoul arrived in Hungary, the German Nazi official Adolf Eichmann had already moved in. He was six years older than Raoul. He was as intent on eliminating Jews, as Raoul was on saving them.

He had joined the Nazi Party in 1932 in Austria where he lived. Six years later, he oversaw the forced eviction and killings of roughly 150,000 Austrian Jews.

The Schutz-Pass

When Raoul entered Hungary in July of 1944, the number of Jews that had already been sent to death camps was estimated at more than 400,000. Somewhere between 180,000 and 230,000 remained in Budapest.

When Raoul arrived in Budapest, he went direct from the train station to the Swedish Legation. There was a long line of Jewish individuals wearing the yellow star and waiting their turn to enter the building. Word had spread that the staff was issuing documents to help with travel and emigration to Sweden.

Raoul already knew one colleague at the office, a diplomat named Per Anger. He briefed Raoul on what the office had done – the issuance of about 700 provisional passports to those with Swedish travel plans or connections.

Raoul proceeded to build on this idea and using his artistic skills designed an elaborate document with the emblem of the Swedish three-crowns, a photograph of the individual and signatures of the ambassador and of Raoul.

This ornate looking document was a Schutz-pass. The text was printed in both German and Hungarian. Referring to the holder of this protective passport, it read in one part:

> "Until his departure, the above-mentioned person and his home are to be regarded as protected by the Royal Swedish Legation in Budapest."
>
> (Reported in "Lost Hero")

Even though there was no real authority or international legislation behind these documents, they were recognized by the Nazis and by Hungary because the passports looked so official.

The Hungarian Foreign Ministry initially gave permission for Raoul to issue 1,500 of the documents, but he negotiated the quantity to 5,000. In reality, many more than those were issued.

Some referred to the Schutz-pass as the "paper of life and death."

Raoul could not increase the number of legitimate passes anymore. Another group started creating counterfeit Swedish passes because they were considered the most respected and valuable. Raoul was in agreement with the counterfeit passes, as long as they remained free and not sold. He wanted to save as many lives as he could.

On 16 July 1944, he wrote his mother the following referencing his former colleague in Sweden:

"Please be so kind and invite Dr. Lauer and his wife. I have learned that his in-laws and evidently also a small child belonging to the family are already dead, i.e., that they have been shipped abroad from Kecskemet – and there they won't stay alive for long."

("Letters And Dispatches 1924-1944 Raoul Wallenberg")

The Arizona Nightclub

In July 1944, Eichmann contacted Raoul and proposed a meeting. He agreed, and they met at the

Arizona Nightclub in Budapest. Raoul wanted to obtain more buildings to place under Swedish protection. Eichmann inquired how many buildings he needed and what he was offering.

Raoul said eventually Sweden would need a minimum of 40 buildings and would pay 200,000 in Swedish currency. Eichmann acknowledged that he had that many already under his control, but expressed surprise that Raoul had not offered more. Raoul wanted the space for his expanding offices and his growing number of employees. He started with 40 staff members, but at its peak, the legation employed 400. The buildings would primarily be used as Swedish Houses.

Safe Houses

Raoul ended up with 30 or more safe houses with a Swedish flag on each one. The Swedish houses served as a refuge for those who had received the Schutz-pass. In addition to the Swedish houses, Switzerland and the International Red Cross set up respective buildings for their protective refugees.

Raoul's relief work extended beyond the Swedish Houses to setting up hospitals. The Jewish population was no longer allowed to go to the existing hospitals. He established soup kitchens and orphanages. Then, through his contacts, he brought in and stored large supplies of food, clothing and medication.

Diplomacy

When it came to diplomacy, Raoul developed his skills to try unconventional methods. Bribery, blackmail, threats and intimidation were sometimes the only tools that worked. He was persistent and patient with the endurance to outlast many opponents.

On 29 September 1944, he included the following in a letter to his mother:

> "About a week ago, I took my official car, a rented Studebaker, and went to a detainment camp on the Austrian border. The commandant refused to receive me at first, then he allotted me five minutes, and finally, after negotiating for four hours, I managed to have 80 people released the very same day and sent to Budapest. It was quite a moving sight."

SUSAN VOLLMER

(Published in "Letters And Dispatches
1924-1944 Raoul Wallenberg")

Arrow Cross Atrocities

On 15 October 1944, while the Hungarian Government tried to seek peace with the Allies, it was overthrown by a Hungarian Nazi group called the Arrow Cross. The Arrow Cross sealed the Jewish houses, and nobody was allowed in or out for 10 days. This resulted in many persons starving to death. The Arrow Cross soldiers did not respect the "protected" houses. Buildings were raided, property stolen, passes destroyed and Jews were murdered.

On 17 October 1944, Raoul went to a synagogue where thousands of Jews were being held captive by the Arrow Cross. Raoul entered the temple and shouted: "Does anyone here have a Swedish protective pass?" Some did. Others said the guards had destroyed them. And others said they had lost theirs, seizing a possible opportunity to escape.

He formed them into lines and told the guards that these were Swedish citizens who they had no authority to detain. He marched hundreds of Jews to his car, where he had a typewriter in the backseat and blank passes to fill in.

The Baroness

On 18 October 1944, the new Hungarian regime announced it would no longer honor passports that Jews held from other nations. That same day, one of Raoul's employees who was also a local publisher arranged a meeting between Raoul and a baroness. She was the newly married wife of the Hungarian foreign minister. She wanted to offer her services with the relief effort.

Raoul advised that she must influence her husband to change the government's position on the protective passes. He said that once the Allies captured Hungary and held trials for war crimes, her husband would be executed.

She wanted to save his life, especially since she was carrying his child. On 20 October 1944, the Hungarian foreign minister convinced the Arrow Cross to honor the protective passes again. He mistakenly believed that this would help gain favor with the neutral countries and increase the chances for recognition as a legitimate government. Later that day, the regime made a radio broadcast for the passports to be honored.

The baroness assisted Raoul's efforts for about six weeks. Then, her husband was advised that she must leave Budapest within 24 hours or face arrest for her activities. She was exiled to her family's home in Italy. The foreign minister said she was taking a recreational trip to the Italian Alps. Raoul, along with the diplomats from other countries came to the train station to see her off.

After everyone else had finished their goodbyes, Raoul went to her compartment and presented flowers to her. They had become extremely close in this short period of time. She cried for having to abandon him and his work.

The Train Station

Raoul was very familiar with the train station. He would find out from an informant when Jews were being grouped and taken to a train station. At the station, they would jam roughly 80 persons into a boxcar or cattle car. If they were lucky, inside the car would be one loaf of bread, eight ounces of jam and a bucket of water for a train ride that would last five days.

When Raoul and a colleague arrived at the station, Raoul would demand that everyone with a Schutz-pass debark from the train. Then, he would assist those who no longer had their passes.

When Jews were boarded onto trains to go to "labor" camps, Raoul would sometimes jump on top of the train. He would hand out the passports to the outstretched hands. Sometimes, the Nazi soldiers would yell or shoot in the direction of Raoul on top of the train. After dismounting the train, he would demand that all of those with the protective passports be allowed to disembark.

"In the name of the government, I demand those with Swedish passports to raise them high," Raoul shouted, according to an article in a New York Times Magazine (30 March 1980). Quick-thinking prisoners would pull out any type of identification, whether it was correct or not. Raoul identified himself as "Wallenberg, Swedish Legation," and told those with passports to come with him. Then, they would quickly climb into the waiting International Red Cross trucks. While riding in the trucks back to Budapest, Raoul and Per Anger filled out a Schutz-pass for each passenger.

For those who didn't have the life-saving pass, they stayed on the train. Some persons went insane during the five-day journey of dehydration and starvation. Others died en route. When they arrived in Poland, they were told they would be given a mug of tea after taking a shower.

In the anteroom, signs indicated to remove all clothing. After everyone entered the showers, the doors were sealed. Instead of water, the showers sprayed Cyanide gas. The gas chamber killed everyone inside within four to five minutes.

Referred to sometimes as "labor" camps, they were really "death" camps. Sometimes the volume was so great that the crematoria could not keep pace.

Death March

In November 1944, the trains were no longer available, so Eichmann decided that marches should be held for about 40,000 Jews. This was a 125-mile (200-kilometer) trip to the Hungarian border. The roadside from Budapest to Hegyeshalom was littered with bodies. More than 10,000 persons died during the march.

Raoul and his staff were able to rescue some along the route, but for the most part, they served as a mobile kitchen, taking food to help alleviate some of the suffering. Before the death marches started, one group was waiting in a brick factory. Raoul had stopped by and said he would be back with doctors and nurses. One survivor said:

"And true to his word, soon afterward some doctors and nurses came from the Jewish hospital. But what stands out most about Raoul Wallenberg is that he came himself. He talked to us, and, most important, he showed that there was a human being who cared about us."

(Reported in the book "Raoul Wallenberg: Angel of Rescue")

The International Ghetto

In Budapest, the city's Jewish population of 60,000 to 70,000 were confined to a Central Ghetto and an International Ghetto. There was no electricity during the freezing cold, so furniture was cut up for firewood, while the residents tried to keep from freezing to death.

Within the ghetto and Budapest itself, other dangers lurked. In a letter to his mother, Raoul wrote, "Thugs are roaming the city, beating, torturing and shooting people. Among my staff alone, there have been 40 cases of kidnapping and beating."

Arrow Cross gangs started taking Jews to the Danube River. They would tie them together in groups of three and shoot the one in the middle. The dead body would pull the other two down into the river, so that they would perish by drowning.

One evening, Raoul asked for some volunteers who could swim to meet him at the river. They parked further downstream from the Arrow Cross. The swimmers rescued 50 people that night from the icy river. Medical staff had also been brought along to treat victims.

On Christmas Eve 1944, the Arrow Cross invaded the children's homes operated by the International Red Cross. Arrow Cross gangs shot some children and then drove others into the Danube, leaving them to drown.

Also on Christmas Eve, Russian soldiers advanced to the outskirts of Buda. Civilians who were in town shopping for presents were cut off from homes in the suburbs. By the day after Christmas, the Soviets surrounded all of Budapest.

Why Meet The Soviets?

In January 1945, Soviet troops marched into Budapest liberating over 80,000 Jews. The Soviets were part of the Allied forces, so Raoul probably felt comfortable meeting with the officers. Several accounts have emerged as to why Raoul wanted to meet with the Soviets. The reports included the following:

- Raoul went to meet with the Russian commander to request food for the Jewish refugees. He said that he had not rescued all of these people to watch them starve.

- Raoul and his staff had written an economic relief plan for the surviving Jewish population. He wanted to share this information with the Soviets as well as details of the humanitarian work done so far.

- Raoul told some of his assistants, "I am going to meet the Russians. I have money with me and will try to help the Jews."

On 13 January 1945, Soviet troops broke through the basement wall of a house where Raoul, his driver and others were staying. The soldiers had been traveling as much as possible through underground tunnels, which connected many Budapest buildings. Some of the tunnels dated back to the Ottoman Empire of the Turks. The underground passages reduced the number of casualties.

After the soldiers emerged from the tunnel, Raoul identified himself as a Swedish diplomat, responsible for protecting Soviet interests during the war. One of the soldiers returned several hours later with higher-ranking officials to question Raoul. He spent the next three days being questioned by the Soviet secret police, known at that time as the NKVD.

When Raoul was released from the questioning, he wanted to prepare for a trip to the Russian headquarters in Hungary. Previously, he had collected 200,000 pengös and some documents from the Swiss Legation that had been kept there for protection. He gave 100,000 pengös to a volunteer for food and protection of the Swedish Jews. He expected that he and his driver would return from the headquarters in seven to eight days. In addition to some of the money, they also concealed in the automobile some of the Jewish valuables of gold and jewelry for safekeeping.

Later on, the Soviets occupied at least one of the Swedish Legation offices. The entire place was ransacked according to Raoul's colleague, Per Anger. The safe was blown up to gain access to its contents. Soldiers shot at paintings for target practice. Curtains were pulled down, and everything of value was removed, including Raoul's files.

On 17 January 1945, Raoul and his driver, Vilmos Langfelder, left for the headquarters of the Soviet occupation forces in Debrecen, approximately 100 to 120 miles east (160 to 192 kilometers) from Budapest. They were escorted by Russian soldiers on motorcycles. However, they never met with the officer in Debrecen.

Although it was not known at that time, it was later uncovered that they were intercepted by the Soviet secret police. He and his driver were taken on a two-week train ride to Moscow and imprisoned in separate cells at Lubyanka Prison. Lubyanka served as both a prison and the headquarters of the Soviet secret police.

Reports agree that an organization involved in Raoul's imprisonment was the NKVD, the Soviet secret police and intelligence agency. In later years, it was known as the KGB and is now referred to as the FSB (Federal Security Service). Although Raoul was a Swedish diplomat from a neutral country, the Soviets believed he was a U.S. spy and / or an agent for Germany.

An in-depth investigation published by U.S. News & World Report (13 May 1996) confirmed that

Raoul was working for the U.S. Office for Strategic Services. This agency was the predecessor of what is now called the Central Intelligence Agency (CIA). Raoul's Swedish diplomatic status and U.S. funds allowed him to rescue thousands upon thousands of Jewish civilians.

There does not seem to be any belief in the theory that he was a double-agent for Germany. One of his relative's businesses sold ball bearings to the Nazis during the war, according to an article in the Minneapolis Star Tribune (16 February 1997). However, there has been no indication that Raoul was involved.

Conflicting Stories

A variety of reports and conflicting stories have emerged over the years since Raoul's disappearance in 1945. Here are the different reports. (Some of the information did not surface for years or decades after it occurred.)

- On <u>16 January 1945</u>, the day before Raoul departed on the trip to Debrecen, the Swedish minister in Moscow received a note. It said that Raoul had been found. "The Russian military authorities have taken measures to protect Raoul Wallenberg and his belongings." (This was reported in the book "Angel Of Rescue.")

- In <u>February 1945</u>, the Russian ambassador in Stockholm, advised Raoul's mother that he was alive and doing well in Russia. The ambassador expected Raoul's return to Sweden. The Soviet authorities viewed this as a blunder, and the ambassador was recalled back to Russia.

- On <u>8 March 1945</u>, a Hungarian radio station broadcast that Raoul was killed by the Nazis on his way to Debrecen (the Soviet field headquarters). The station was Soviet controlled, and many did not consider this a reliable report.

- From <u>April 1945 to spring 1947</u>, Raoul was believed to have been held in the Lefortovskaya Prison in Moscow, after his initial stay at Lubyanka.

- On <u>18 August 1947</u>, the deputy foreign minister of the Soviet Union stated that "Wallenberg is not in the Soviet Union and is unknown to us."

- In <u>1948</u>, Raoul was one of the person's nominated for a Nobel Peace Prize by members of the Swedish, British and Uruguayan parliaments. Professors from Denmark and Israel also nominated him. No one was awarded a peace prize that year. The commission stated that no "living individual worthy of the prize" had been found.

- From spring 1949 to January 1953, it was reported that Raoul was held in different prisons located in Siberia. This included the prisons of Vorkuta, Khal'mer Yu and Verkhneural'sk.

- From 1953 to 1960, Raoul is believed to have been held in the Moscow prisons of Vladimir and Butyrka.

- In February 1957, the Soviets announced finding a document, which stated that, the prisoner "Walenberg" (misspelled in note) died in his cell of a believed heart attack. (The note dated 17 July 1947 means that Raoul would have suffered a heart attack at the age of 36.)

- In January of 1961, Dr. Nanna Svartz who was the Swedish physician of Raoul's mother was attending a medical conference in Moscow. She spoke with a Soviet specialist she already knew named Professor Aleksandr Miasnikov. He advised that Raoul was in poor condition and in a Soviet mental hospital. He later recanted the remarks saying he didn't understand due to his inadequate German language skills. He said this verbally, put it in a letter and then repeated it four years later in a meeting with foreign office representatives.

- In <u>1961</u>, Raoul was transferred to Wrangell Island Prison, about 300 miles (480 kilometers) inside of the Arctic Circle, 100 miles (160 kilometers) north of Siberia.

- In <u>1965</u>, the Swedish doctor Svartz returned to Moscow and saw the Soviet doctor she knew. This time, he told her that Raoul had died recently. He was tired, depressed and possibly went on a hunger strike. The Soviet doctor died suddenly in 1965. (The Swedish doctor did not share this information with the public until 1981.)

- In <u>November 1977</u>, Simon Wiesenthal spoke regarding human rights violations in Russia and Eastern Europe. He said that Raoul had been seen as late as 1975 in a mental hospital in Siberia.

- In <u>1979</u>, a U.S. Free Wallenberg Committee was formed by Congressional Representative Tom Lantos, and his wife, Annette, who were each saved separately from the Nazis in Hungary. The committee included U.S. senators who worked with other groups in England, France, Israel, Switzerland and even West Germany.

- In <u>1980</u>, it was reported that Raoul was in the Mordvinia Prison, located in the republic of

Moldavia. There was a special section for prisoners who had been declared "officially missing or dead" by the Russian government.

- In August <u>1991</u>, then Russian President Mikhail Gorbachov authorizes an investigation. It is determined that Raoul died in a Russian prison. However, the file is missing.

- On <u>22 November 1991</u>, the top aide to the head of the KGB Vadim Bakatin suggested that Raoul had been executed by the Soviets. Before all the information could be obtained, Boris Yeltsin took over in January 1992 and access to KGB files was denied to the outside. This seems to have continued, as the FSB has been comprised of key former KGB staff.

- In <u>April 1992</u>, a KGB archivist accidentally found Raoul's passport and personal belongings in an envelope. This was in a room that was previously used as part of the Lubyanka Prison in Moscow.

- In <u>1994</u>, a former Soviet spy, Pavel Sudoplatov, wrote a book published in the United States titled "Special Tasks." His theory was that the Soviets tried to recruit Raoul to be an agent for the U.S.S.R. or else they would expose him in regard to their beliefs that he was a double-agent for Germany. Instead of Palestine, the Kremlin wanted the Jewish state to be established in the Crimea, now part of the Ukraine. Raoul was designated to raise the international capital needed for the Jewish homeland and for postwar economic reconstruction. From 1945 to 1947, they tried unsuccessfully to make Raoul betray his country and himself. In 1947, it was determined he should be liquidated. Raoul was poisoned by injection of a toxicological substance. He was cremated without an autopsy.

Eichmann After World War II

After World War II ended, charges of war crimes were brought and held in Nuremberg, Germany. International law created a new charge known as "crimes against humanity." This meant that anyone charged with this crime could not claim as a defense that he was only following orders from a superior.

One of the persons who got away after the war ended was Adolf Eichmann. He escaped to Argentina in 1950. He reunited with his family and worked as a mechanic, while also overseeing a rabbit farm. Many people never forgot his role in the Holocaust. In 1960, Israeli agents found him. Since formal extraditions were not available with Argentina,

Israeli agents captured him and brought him to Jerusalem by kidnapping him.

Once there, he was charged with crimes against the Jewish people. During the trial, he sat in a bulletproof box. They did not want him assassinated before the trial ended. Eichmann was convicted. The execution by hanging occurred on 31 May 1962.

The Foundation

In the name of Raoul Wallenberg, an international foundation was created to develop educational programs about the Holocaust. The non-profit organization has offices in New York, Jerusalem and Buenos Aires, Argentina.

Where's The Proof?

Because so many reports and theories exist about Raoul, there is no agreed upon answer because there has been no proof. It does seem definite that he was in the Soviet prison system. Was there no one else, other than Raoul himself, who understood that to rescue someone may require a diplomacy of bribery, threats and intimidation? The thought is too much to bear that the man who rescued so many from certain death was never rescued himself.

RAOUL WALLENBERG (Sweden)		
Born: 4 August 1912	Died: (unknown)	Age: (unknown)
"If people have such great expectations, then it can only help them. From their faith and confidence, they'll gain the strength to resist. If they believe the passes are legitimate and powerful, then they may convince others, even the police, that they're powerful. The confidence and faith of the Jews here has given us all strength. It gives me strength." ~ Raoul Wallenberg (Reported in the book "Lost Hero")		

ROBERT CAPA

One year before the start of the first World War, Endre Friedmann was born in 1913 in Budapest, Hungary. At that time, the area comprised two cities on opposite sites of the Danube River. "Buda" built among the hills served as the seat of government and had the palaces of the wealthy German families. The "Pest" side served as the artistic and intellectual community. Located on flat land, it had a liberal Jewish middle class. Appearances were important in Pest with its citizens striving to project an image beyond their means.

Endre was appropriately born on the Pest side of Budapest to a Jewish family. Upon his birth, it was taken as a favorable sign that he was born with an extra pinky on one hand. The sixth finger was surgically removed. His mother, Julia, knew her second son was special and would become a famous man. His parents operated a fashionable clothing business. His mother was a hard-working, strong-willed businesswoman. While his dad, as co-owner and head tailor, preferred to rely on his charm and connections. He enjoyed staying out late to play cards. His father, Dezsö, loved to tell stories, especially of his wanderlust. He left his Transylvania home as a youth to travel through Europe, including the cities of London and Paris, and he used his wits and street smarts to get by.

In October 1929, the American stock market crash reverberated around the world – disrupting the Hungarian economy as well. Customers had less money to spend on new clothes. Instead of having a separate store, the Friedmanns now operated the clothing business out of their own apartment. The bedrooms for the three boys (László, Endre and Cornel) were converted to workrooms.

Endre began spending more time away from home. During business hours, the Friedmanns could have from 20 to 40 employees plus customers in the apartment. For privacy, Endre retreated to the bathroom, spending several hours in the bath reading.

In Berlin, Germany

One of Endre's childhood friends, Eva Besnyö, was about three years older than him. She loved photography and was aware of the trend to use photos for social consciousness. She went to Berlin to study photography.

About a year later, Endre also went to Berlin, arriving in September 1931 to attend college for the winter session. After a while, his parents were no longer able to send him money. He needed to find a job, and his German language skills were not too good.

Photography appealed to him and would allow him to go into journalism without being fluent in German. His friend, Eva, placed Endre in touch with some of her contacts. She helped him obtain his first photography job as an assistant at a photo agency called Dephot.

Endre gave up on college but not on his photography. At Dephot, he worked as a darkroom assistant, arranged assignments and did office work. He was allowed to fill in on a shooting assignment and borrowed a Leica camera. Endre was to photograph a speech given by Leon Trotsky, a Russian revolutionary leader, at a 1932 social democratic conference in Copenhagen. This fueled his interest in photography. In the meantime, Adolf Hitler and Nazism began growing in Germany, which led Endre to move to Paris in 1933.

In Paris

After arriving in Paris, Endre began spelling his name as "André." He and his roommate moved from one rundown hotel to another because they were unable to pay.

André tried to find work, but the competition was intense. There were more photographers than assignments. Plus, his portfolio was limited.

When things were really bad, he would dissolve sugar in water as a drink to help curb his hunger. He also periodically pawned his camera. This was extremely depressing because he feared a life of poverty and hunger with no means to make a living.

Gerda

Through the staff he had previously worked with in Berlin, André started to receive some work. First, it was printing photos. Then, he received a photo assignment in September 1934 calling for photographs of a blond blue-eyed girl on a park bench to be used by a life insurance company.

In search of a model, André went to a cafe and found an excellent candidate. The young woman, named Ruth Cerf, agreed. Ruth brought along her roommate so that she would feel more comfortable in meeting with the photographer. Her roommate, named Gerda Pohorylles came to the photo shoot, held at a park with many trees in Montparnasse. Located in south central Paris, it was noted for artistic and bohemian life.

Barely over five feet tall, Gerda was vivacious with an intense personality. Even though she didn't have any money, she still came across as quite elegant.

Gerda worked part time as a secretary for a child psychiatrist. Her roommate who didn't make much money either worked at an organization to help immigrants. To save on food, they would stay in bed on Sundays and read, instead of eating.

Gerda had a boyfriend who was attending college to study medicine. Gerda and André became close friends. She took on the role as manager of his freelance assignments. From a development standpoint, she made suggestions on how he could improve his appearance from grooming to how he dressed. Her encouragement made him more serious about work and helped him analyze story ideas. André listened to her and even called her "the boss." She helped him focus his life and gave it direction – direction that he had missed in his earlier years.

In January 1935, his mom had sisters living in the United States in New York. She decided to scout out the situation as a place to live. Her eldest son had died about six months earlier due to a rheumatic heart condition.

That summer of 1935, André photographed Bastille Day celebrations in Marseilles, a port city in southeast France. Then, he traveled to Cannes, a beautiful Mediterranean resort area. André went there to meet Gerda, her now ex-boyfriend and another student from the medical school. A few miles offshore from Cannes, they stayed on an island named Sainte-Marguerite. It was believed to be the island where an heir to the throne (known as the "Man In The Iron Mask") had been imprisoned.

They camped, explored the ruins and swam. They ate canned sardines. Over the summer, he and Gerda fell in love. He described it as the happiest time in his life.

Robert "Bob" Capa

Gerda and André created a plan to increase the cost of his photos and to build a persona. There already was an established photographer in Paris whose last name was Friedmann and first name Georges.

Since many publications then only used a last name on a photo credit, it would be impossible to tell André's work from the other photographer's.

Gerda and André felt there were more opportunities for Americans. They created a fictitious person named Robert "Bob" Capa, a wealthy American photographer who commanded higher prices for his work. Gerda served as the salesperson and the secretary for the photo association. André handled the darkroom work, and his alter ego, Robert Capa, shot the photographs. When editors saw André shooting photos and then turning them in as Robert Capa's, they knew he was the same person.

André took over the Robert Capa name and would strive to live up to the persona. The name change did increase Robert Capa's photo cost two to three times more than André's.

Gerda changed her last name to Taro. The name came from a Japanese painter and was easier to spell and say than Pohorylles. In addition to being his agent, Gerda learned the art of photography from Robert. They received an assignment from the French magazine Vu to go together and document the Spanish Civil War.

The Spanish Civil War

It was literally a crash landing when they arrived in Spain. For a special issue of Vu magazine, a team of journalists had been assembled. While flying over the Pyrenees, the plane lost altitude. The pilot crash-landed the plane in a field outside of Barcelona. Amazingly, a few people broke their arms, but that was all. Robert and Gerda were not injured and able to use their cameras to photograph the war.

Before the war, Spain had recently awakened as an emerging country with arts, freedom, labor unions and an enlightened social party. However, this changed when the country was overtaken by its own military.

At about the same time as the Spanish Civil War, technical advancements in film speed and the use of 35-mm cameras led to the development of photojournalism in the mass media. This was the first war to become primarily known through still photography. One of Robert's most famous photographs was taken in Spain when he was only 22.

The photo is believed to have been captured on 5 September 1936 on the Córdoba front, a province located in southern Spain. Called "Death of a Loyalist Soldier," it shows Federico Borrell Garcia who has just been shot, falling backward with his arm outstretched – about to drop the rifle as he makes the transition from life to death. It is a moment frozen in time that the human eye could not have completely perceived, but the camera captured on film.

Photographs shot by Robert and Gerda included – the militia camping and helping farmers to harvest crops when things were slow. They continued to shoot photos of combat but also people in cafes, soldiers at train stations, kids trying to play on city barricades and churches that had been burned by mobs. The effect of war on civilians was also shown. This included women forced to live with bombings, starvation, loss of homes and deaths of loved ones.

Gerda began to receive recognition for her photography skills as well, and this helped fuel her independence. She not only encouraged Robert to take risks but also wanted to go with him.

In the spring of 1937, Robert asked Gerda to marry him. However, she declined. She now offered him more freedom than love.

As Robert's professional connections grew, he no longer used an agent. As a result, he needed to return to Paris to sell their photographs. Gerda was scheduled to join Robert in Paris. He was also setting up an assignment that would take them to China for Life magazine.

On the day before her scheduled departure for Paris, Gerda wanted to take some more photos at Brunete, where Republican soldiers were reclaiming some territory. Gerda saw this as her last chance to get even better action photos before leaving. She set out with a companion Ted Allan arriving at the general's headquarters on the Brunete front. The general wanted them to leave immediately due to the danger, but Gerda would not go. They took cover in a foxhole, and she started shooting with her camera as planes flew overhead, dropping bombs.

After the bombings at the end of the afternoon, they headed out on foot. When they saw the general's car, they stopped it. He wasn't inside, but there were wounded men in the back seat. Gerda put her cameras in the front seat. Then, she and Ted jumped on the running board.

While on the running board, a Loyalist tank appeared to be out of control heading in their direction. The driver of the car swerved, but the tank accidentally sideswiped the vehicle. Gerda suffered internal injuries. She was taken to a hospital and operated on. She died on the day she was to return to Paris. Her companion recovered.

Robert heard the news while in Paris. Devastated and heartbroken, he did not return to Spain for five months. Democracy lost in the Spanish Civil War as Hitler sent in armaments to help Francisco Franco, the Spanish dictator.

The Anti-War Photographer

This was the first war Robert would cover, but it would not be the last. Amazingly, he photographed active combat in five wars:

- The Spanish Civil War (1936-1939)
- The Sino-Japanese War (1938)
- World War II--European Theater (1941-1945)
- First Arab-Israeli War (1948)
- The French Indochina War (1954)

Due to his assignments, Robert often became described as a war photographer. However, it would be more appropriate to call him an anti-war photographer. "He was a pacifist, and he wrote once that he felt like a hyena pursuing desolation around the world," according to Peter Clowney, reporter for National Public Radio in Philadelphia.

In 1938, Robert was already being praised as one of the greatest photographers. His photos were done with compassion, as he tried to retain the dignity and the tragedy of those affected by war. His fame was bittersweet without Gerda there to share it.

World War II

Robert Capa became one of four photographers and reporters selected to cover the invasion. The Allied forces had divided the Normandy coast of France into different sections and would arrive in the largest armada ever assembled.

In preparing for the trip, Robert packed two cameras and film. He kept the film dry by placing the canisters inside rubber condoms. He had learned that soldiers used condoms to protect their ammunition out in the field. He made sure to take brandy. Plus, he would need cigarettes and cards for poker playing. And he also brought a raincoat.

On 6 June 1944, a U.S. ship arrived off the Normandy shore in what has been described as "the longest day." Breakfast was served about 3 a.m. by staff in white jackets. The meal included hotcakes, sausages, eggs and coffee to fortify the men for the assault, and for many, it was their last meal.

The tide was low. Soldiers went to the debarkation area and boarded landing craft for a 12-mile trip to the beach. Waves rose three to six feet high and crashed on the crafts drenching the men with water.

The landing craft opened its door for the soldiers and photographer to depart. They carried their rifles above their head, and he raised his camera. Hundreds of men died in minutes from German artillery fire.

Robert made his way through the seawater past vomit and dead bodies. He let go of his raincoat and allowed it to float off into the sea. He felt that he no longer needed it.

He took cover for a while behind a partially burnt amphibious tank. Then, he ran behind two soldiers to the beach.

He shot a roll of film in each of his two cameras. When he finished the photos, he saw a landing craft with Red Cross medics disembarking into the water. He made his way to the landing craft, which was returning to the big ship. The decks were already full of wounded and dead soldiers.

Robert wrote later in his book "Images Of War:"

> "The mess boys who had served our coffee in white jackets and with white gloves at three in the morning were covered with blood and were sewing the dead in white sacks."

On 8 June 1944, Robert returned to Omaha Beach. Instead of gunfire, temporary graves were being dug, and a funeral service was being held.

That evening, he found his press colleagues holding a wake in his memory! A sergeant had reported seeing Robert Capa's body afloat in the sea. Since he had been gone 48 hours from the front line, he was pronounced officially deceased.

Now, the wake was a celebration that he was still alive. He drank several bottles of apple brandy with correspondent Ernie Pyle and Charles Wertenbaker, head of Time and Life's European staff.

Once again, Robert Capa made it through and had shot 72 images. At that time, he was taking photos for Life magazine. The film went to London for processing. By accident, the majority of the negatives melted because the doors were closed on the drying cabinet to speed the processing. Only 11 pictures were even salvageable and those appeared blurred.

Moments Of Truth

Anyone trained in photography knows that the goal is to capture the moment of truth. It is that instance when someone drops all facades – when the most important part of an action occurs. Robert captured many moments of truth through his skill and his sensitivity.

He shot photographs of his famous friends – writer Ernest Hemingway, painter Pablo Picasso with his family, actor Gary Cooper and actress Ingrid Bergman.

Ingrid Bergman

Since Gerda's death, Robert had been involved with different women – some more seriously than others.

He had even entered into a marriage of convenience that was not consummated but kept him from being deported from the United States. It gave him the U.S. passport he needed to continue his work.

While in Paris, Robert was talking to correspondent Irwin Shaw in the Ritz Hotel lobby, when Ingrid Bergman checked in. They decided to send her a note. They said they would like to invite her to dinner. Or, they could send her flowers, but they did not have enough money for both. She accepted, and she joined them for dinner with more of their friends for an evening of laughter and dancing.

Robert and Ingrid were each working on assignments in Berlin when they met again. Their friendship grew, and they returned to Paris. They went sightseeing, drank champagne and went to corner bars. She would write in her memoirs that she fell in love with Robert in Paris.

She could see beyond his debonair persona of the foreign correspondent. When he slept, he had nightmares of the images of death and violence that he had seen.

Like a soldier, he suffered from the aftereffects of not just one but three wars to date. He was restless, depressed and irritable. He drank too much, lacked focus and suffered from survivor's guilt. Ingrid spoke of leaving her husband for Robert, but he did not encourage her, despite their love. A life with her would also mean much time in Hollywood, California, in the United States. He had gone there before and not enjoyed it. He decided to try Hollywood again – this time to write about his experiences in war as a screenplay. Once there, he could not focus on his writing.

They each took separate trips to New York and met while they were there. During this time, Robert was sworn in to become a citizen of the United States.

On friendly terms, they agreed to end their affair while taking a vacation in Sun Valley, Idaho. Robert then went to the casino and gambled away all of his savings, about $2,000 U.S. dollars.

A Toast To Magnum

Several years after World War II ended, Robert and a group of photographers including Henri Cartier-Bresson founded a photo agency in 1947. It was an idea that Robert had considered since 1938. Now, it was time to make it happen.

At a brainstorming meeting on establishing the agency, a magnum of champagne was popped open. Someone yelled "Magnum," and the name of the photo agency was chosen. The name implies glamour but also a connotation for toughness due to a gun by the same name. Plus, the Latin definition means greatness.

The idea was to bring photographers together, where they would be stronger as a group, rather than as individuals. They advocated that photographers should own the copyright of the photos they take, much like book authors do with printed material.

The agency opened offices in Paris and in New York. In addition to the members, Robert created the idea of associates who were freelancers. These photographers would not own shares but they could use the Magnum name in their photo credits.

One associate named Ernest Haas, told Robert that he needed to look for a traditional journalism job because he was running out of money.

Robert, who was known for living beyond his means, contemplated the situation while playing poker that night. Fortunately, it happened to be a winning night for him. When he visited Ernest in his hotel room, he threw all the money up in the air in a dramatic gesture stating that it was for Ernest, so he could stay with Magnum.

The Rebirth Of A Nation

In the aftermath of World War II, the British decided to leave what was then called Palestine, and a homeland was to be created for the Jewish population. Of Jewish descent, Robert wanted to cover the rebirth of the nation of Israel. He approached Life magazine, but the editor had already assigned three photographers. He received a commitment from a magazine called Illustrated and headed out to Tel Aviv on 8 May 1948.

Many expected a war after the British planned departure had been set for 14 May 1948. Robert shot Israel's first cabinet meeting that day and the ecstatic crowds in the streets. That evening, several Arab states attacked Israel.

The Arabs cut the road to Tel Aviv from Jerusalem, which was the only route for food and other necessities. It was urgent to find a way to transport supplies to Jerusalem.

A walking path was found in the area that went through the mountains linking the two cities. The government approved a plan to widen the trail into a usable path for vehicles. Engineers and laborers with bulldozers went in. Crews worked 24 hours a day amid sniper and artillery fire until the Burma Road could be used – about a week later.

Bitter Rice

After Israel, Robert was later working on assignment in Japan. That was when an editor at Life magazine contacted Magnum about another assignment. The current Life photographer had to leave Indochina because his mother had suffered a heart attack. Could Robert fill in?

About 9 May 1954, Robert landed in Hanoi, Indochina (now divided into the countries of Vietnam, Laos and Cambodia). The Viet Minh had said that approximately 750 wounded French prisoners of war could be evacuated.

He shot photos of the injured soldiers being placed on planes. He also covered a tent city where exhausted French soldiers had retreated, also waiting for transport.

Robert and Time-Life correspondent John Mecklin flew together to Nam Dinh in the Red River Delta, located 45 miles (72 kilometers) southeast of Hanoi.

SUSAN VOLLMER

John Mecklin wrote the following about Robert, published in the book "Images Of War."

"On his delta tour, Capa had got the idea of a picture story to be entitled 'Bitter Rice.' His plan was to dramatize the contrast of tanks next to peasants working in the paddies, of men dying in the struggle for the rice harvest. All morning he worked to photograph peasants carrying rice to market in straw baskets, plodding along the edges of vehicle-clogged roads."

After taking photos that morning, Robert napped at lunch time. About 2:50 p.m. that afternoon, he announced that he was going to walk up the road. Firing was going on in every direction. Others thought it too dangerous, but he still wanted to go. He said to let him know when it was time to move out.

About 15 minutes later, a Vietnamese soldier came up and said in Vietnamese, "The photographer is dead." Near the foot of a dike, they found Robert Capa on his back. His left leg was gone after stepping on a land mine. In addition, he had suffered an extensive chest wound. He died with his camera still clutched in his left hand. He became the first Life photographer to be killed in the line of duty. His body was brought to a Quaker Cemetery, called Amawalk Friends Cemetery, about 30 miles north of Purchase, New York. Stenciled on the rough wooden coffin were the words:

Robert Capa, Photographe, Mort En Indochine

(Robert Capa, Photographer, Died In Indochina)

In his memory, the Overseas Press Club established the Robert Capa Award. The award is for "superlative photography requiring exceptional courage and enterprise abroad."

After Robert's death, his brother Cornell joined Magnum to help ensure its survival and the preservation of his brother's legacy. Robert's legacy includes:

- The concept that photographers should own the copyright to their work.
- The extensive collection he created of historical photographs.

Robert Capa lived and documented the images of many persons in intense circumstances. He was a master not just of photography but of living in the moment.

ROBERT CAPA (Hungary)		
Born: 22 October 1913	Died: 25 May 1954	Age: 40
"It's not easy always to stand aside and be unable to do anything except record the sufferings around one." ~ Robert Capa (Reported in his book "Images Of War")		

MARTIN LUTHER KING JR.

Michael King Jr. was born into a legacy of Baptist preachers. Yet, no one knew at the time, he would become the most influential of them all. He combined his religious beliefs with a conviction for justice that propelled the civil rights movement.

On 15 January 1929, Michael Jr. was born in Atlanta to Alberta Williams King and Michael King Sr. Five years later, the father decided to change his name and his son's name to Martin Luther, as a tribute to the founder of Protestant Christianity.

In his early years, Martin Luther King Jr. was called by his initials, M.L. His family support, church and educational opportunities gave him a good start in life. He entered nursery school at the age of three and kindergarten at the age of five.

One of Martin's best childhood friends was white and was about his same age. His friend's dad owned a store across the street from the house. They played childhood games together. At the age of six, it was time for the boys to enter elementary school. Martin found out they would attend separate schools. Years later, in a college essay paper, he wrote about the experience:

> "The climax came when he told me one day that his father had demanded that he would play with me no more. I never will forget what a great shock this was to me."

(From "The Papers of Martin Luther King Jr.")

Later, he would tell his parents about the incident at the dinner table. That was the first time he became aware of a racial issue but certainly not the last.

Through his education, Martin skipped several grades. He entered the 10th grade of public high school when he was only 13 years old. In his second year of high school, he won a public speaking contest, enabling him to compete on a state level. The contest, sponsored by the black Elks, was held in Dublin, Georgia. Riding the bus home from the competition, the black students were expected to give up their seats when white passengers boarded. The students refused. The bus driver cursed at them. When their speech teacher warned them about the potential dangers, they gave up their seats. Standing during the return trip to Atlanta, Martin experienced one of the angriest moments in his life.

College Education

In 1944, he attended Atlanta's all-black Morehouse College at the age of 15. Unlike most college students, he lived at home. He clashed with his father over the right to dance and with his father's attitude that his way was the only way.

He considered becoming a lawyer at this time. But two instructors at the college influenced him. They showed how relevant the stories in the Bible are of oppressed people struggling for salvation.

Martin understood that he could preach the Gospel and lead people to justice at the same time.

In the fall of 1948, Martin entered Crozer Theological Seminary in Chester, Pennsylvania. At the age of 19, he was one of 11 black students in a college of 90 attendees. While most of his grades were A's and B's, it's hard to believe now that he received a C in public speaking.

In 1951, at the age of 22, he graduated valedictorian with a bachelor's degree in divinity. He received a scholarship and selected Boston University for his graduate studies. While in Boston, he studied religion in greater detail. But he also made time to dine out and have fun at the jazz clubs.

Through a mutual friend, Martin heard about a young woman who was studying voice and singing at the New England Conservatory of Music. Like Martin, she attended college up north but her family was in the south.

Martin called Coretta Scott to introduce himself and to ask her out to lunch. They dated for over a year. At first, she was reluctant to set aside her dreams of being a professional singer to become a preacher's wife. However, she did. Coretta and Martin married on 18 June 1953 outside her parents' home in Marion, Alabama.

The Move To Montgomery

At the age of 25, Martin and his wife went to Montgomery, Alabama, where he would finish his doctoral thesis. He also had an opportunity to preach a sermon at the Dexter Avenue Baptist Church.

His sermon focused on the importance of leading a loving and balanced life as a Christian. Afterward, the congregation offered him the job as pastor, which he accepted.

On 1 December 1955, an event happened which propelled Martin from minister to activist. It was the holiday season, and Rosa Parks finished a long day of tailoring and ironing at a department store.

On her way home, she carried a bag of groceries and boarded a city bus. She sat in the midsection between the "whites only" and the "colored" section in the rear. It was an accepted practice for blacks to sit in this section if the rear was full.

A white man boarded the bus at a stop, and the driver ordered Rosa and three other blacks to vacate that area, so the white passenger could have it all. While the others moved, Rosa did not.

The bus company and city officials were approached to allow all passengers, regardless of race, to obtain a seat on a first-come, first-served basis and also to hire some black bus drivers. The proposals were not accepted, so the black community began a boycott of the bus service and asked Martin to become the official spokesperson.

Instead of using the bus, blacks walked or used a group car pool. Volunteers who had cars picked up riders to take them to work and later to go home. The days of the boycott turned into weeks and then into months. Officials began arresting car pool drivers for minor offenses. Others received notice that their vehicle insurance had been canceled.

Martin and his family continually received abusive letters and calls. Sometimes, there were 40 phone calls a day threatening their lives. On 30 January 1956, a bomb exploded on the porch of the King's home. Martin was at the church, but his wife and daughter were at home. Fortunately, they were not injured.

To the media, Martin made a statement: "I did not start this boycott. I was asked by you to serve as your spokesman. I want it to be known the length and breadth of this land that if I am stopped, this movement will not stop."

While the bus boycott continued, a federal court case had been filed claiming that bus segregation was unconstitutional. On 13 November 1956, the U.S. Supreme Court declared Alabama's bus segregation illegal. A little over a month later, the court ruling became law in Montgomery. The bus boycott ended more than one year later after it began. The boycott lasted 381 days, ending on 20 December 1956.

After the bus boycott ended, Martin wrote his first of seven books. While signing copies of his book in New York City, a deranged black woman stabbed him in the chest with a letter opener. He would have died the doctor said later if he had sneezed before his condition was stabilized.

'Ghost Of Gandhi'

As Martin continued his activism and civil rights work, he incorporated a policy of non-violence. This tied in well with his Christian beliefs. He also believed that blacks could not win in a violent confrontation against armed authorities.

In 1956, The New Republic magazine referred to "the ghost of Gandhi" as the peaceful resistance that was being used in the south. Mahatma Gandhi led the non-violent movement, which brought about the end of British rule in India.

Martin and numerous African Americans employed sit-ins at lunch counters, libraries and churches. The National Association for the Advancement of Colored People (NAACP) worked to defend those arrested during sit-ins. While Martin was a key figure in the civil rights movement, not all blacks accepted him or his techniques. More militant extremists such as Malcolm X advocated violent techniques.

In his style of leadership, Martin would listen during meetings while others argued. After the debate, he would summarize the views and look for a path to move forward. He tried not to sever ties with anyone who might help the cause.

To help in the fight with segregation, Martin formed the Southern Christian Leadership Conference (SCLC) in 1957. Two years later, he and his family moved to Atlanta, so he could direct the activities of the organization. In 1960, he joined his dad to become co-pastor of the Ebenezer Baptist Church, which he had attended as a child.

Letter From Birmingham Jail

In 1963, Martin along with other ministers held a sit-in against segregated public facilities. After his arrest on 12 April 1963, Martin wrote what is called "Letter From Birmingham Jail" four days later. Here is an excerpt:

> "I have heard numerous southern religious leaders admonish their worshipers to comply with a desegregation decision because it is the law, but I have longed to hear white

> ministers declare: 'Follow this decree because integration is morally right and because the Negro is your brother.' "
>
> ~ Martin Luther King Jr.
>
> Stanford University site, (www.stanford.edu)

I Have A Dream

The pinnacle of the civil rights movement came on 28 August 1963 at the largest demonstration of its kind. In the days leading up to the event, buses, private vehicles, planes and trains started heading to their destination in Washington, D.C.

The caravans themselves caused much anticipation. Those who couldn't attend gathered along roads to cheer those going. Some activists traveled as long as six days to participate.

Those marching assembled at the Washington Monument. An estimated 250,000 activists came which reached from the Washington Monument to the Lincoln Memorial, where Martin gave his speech.

The speech had been positioned as the "march on Washington for jobs and freedom." It turned into the "I have a dream" speech. Those who had a copy of his prepared remarks knew that Martin had left the text.

His inspired vision of what America could be brought new hope.

Here is an excerpt from the speech:

> "I have a dream that one day, on the red hills of Georgia, sons of former slaves and the sons of former slave owners will be able to sit down together at the table of brotherhood. ..."
>
> "I have a dream that my four little children will one day live in a nation where they will not be judged by the color of their skin but by the content of their character."
>
> (From "The Words Of Martin Luther King, Jr.")

His message of hope helped with pending legislation for a civil rights bill. The peaceful tone and demonstration positioned Martin as a moderate in the civil rights struggle.

On 2 July 1964, President Lyndon B. Johnson signed the Civil Rights Act into law. That same year, Martin would win the Nobel Peace Price.

The Nobel Peace Price

Even during his most influential period, Martin suffered from depression that was compounded by fame and pressure. To accept the Nobel Prize, Martin traveled to Oslo, Norway. His public persona still remained engaging.

The prize money came to $54,000. His wife, Coretta, wanted part of the money set aside as a college fund for their children. Martin felt it should go back into the organizations that had worked with him. This meant $37,000 to the Southern Christian Leadership Conference and $17,000 to participating groups in the Council for the United Civil Rights Leadership.

Fortunately, later on, singer Harry Belafonte established a scholarship fund for Martin and Coretta's children.

It was believed that the head of the FBI at that time attempted to discredit Martin. A smear campaign began involving allegations of Communist sympathies, promiscuity and financial wrongdoing.

The Marches On Selma

Voting rights had become an important issue due to discrimination and unnecessary barriers when blacks attempted to register to vote. Martin had even met with President Johnson to encourage a voting rights bill. To draw attention to the situation, a march was planned for Selma, Alabama.

Governor George Wallace made clear his viewpoint in advance that no march would be allowed. Martin advocated postponing the march. However, others in the organization wanted to hold it because an estimated 500 to 600 persons had still arrived to participate.

Without Martin, the protest went forward on 7 March 1965 from a chapel through the streets of Selma to the Edmund Pettus Bridge. At the bridge, they saw Alabama state troopers and white civilians waving Confederate flags.

One of the state troopers ordered them to return to the church or their homes. After unsuccessfully trying to discuss the situation, the leaders of the march and those at the front knelt and prayed. The troopers moved in on the marchers using nightsticks and then tear gas.

It was decided that a second march would be held and the date was two days later – 9 March 1965. Martin contacted churches to join them in a march for freedom. To avoid another violent confrontation from the state troopers, federal authorities suggested an abbreviated march – one that would go only to the bridge and then return.

The second march drew 1,500 demonstrators, more than double the first group. The marchers sang and then knelt in prayer as the group stretched across the bridge and back into Selma.

The second march remained peaceful, and national attention focused on voting rights.

The Move To Chicago

Martin and his family moved to a slum tenement in Chicago. He wanted to support a fellow activist Jesse Jackson in his efforts to improve conditions for the poor. In 1966, the slums were extensive. Absentee landlords operated many of the dilapidated buildings.

Being confined to a slum area perpetuated gangs. Gang members carried weapons and would terrorize those in their own neighborhoods. These youths had no respect for the church, and they seemed unable to reach them.

On 27 November 1967, Martin promoted a campaign to benefit poor people. Washington, D.C., became the targeted destination again to advocate legislation.

I Am A Man

Before the D.C. march, a pressing need arose in Memphis. On 31 January 1968, management sent sanitation workers home due to the rain. White employees received a full day's pay. Black employees received two hours of pay. The blacks held a strike for better pay and for improved working conditions. Strike leaders sought Martin's support. On 28 March 1968, the demonstration was held in the streets of Memphis. Sanitation workers wore posters stating: "I Am A Man."

During the march, a militant group of protesters known as the Invaders left the walk and started looting stores along the way. When the violence started, one of the leaders and organizers of the peaceful protest – the Rev. James Lawson – stopped the march. Martin and his close advisers were just leaving the scene as the police moved in. In the aftermath, a 16-year-old member of the Invaders was shot and killed by police.

Plus, an estimated 60 persons received wounds, primarily from nightsticks.

After leaving Memphis, Martin decided to show that a non-violent march could still be held. He returned on 3 April 1968. In the days leading up to the March, Martin gave the following speech:

> "He's allowed me to go up to the mountain. And I've looked over. And I've seen the promised land. I may not get there with you. But I want you to know tonight that we as a people will get to the promised land."
>
> (From "The Words Of Martin Luther King, Jr.")

The following day, while staying at the Lorraine Motel, he worked with his colleagues to plan the particulars of the march. Then, it was time to head out for dinner. While out on the balcony of the motel, in preparation to leave, a sniper shot Martin with a rifle. Martin was transported to the hospital where he died within the hour.

While one person was convicted for the crime and has since died while in prison, many believe a conspiracy was behind the assassination. Martin's own family believed another person was responsible and sued him in civil court and won. This man owned a bar across the street from the motel and has since died.

Martin's funeral took place at his own Ebenezer Baptist Church. A simple farm wagon pulled by mules transported the coffin to a memorial service at his local alma mater – Morehouse College.

Afterward

On 8 April 1968, the march in Memphis was held for the sanitation workers and for Martin Luther King Jr. About 100,000 persons joined in the march.

The Poor People's Campaign moved forward with a march on Washington, D.C. on 13 May 1968. In addition to the march, approximately 5,000 activists created a makeshift residence on the mall of the Lincoln Memorial. This symbolized the plight of all poor people with participation from blacks, whites, Latinos and Native Americans.

The temporary village was known as "Resurrection City."

MARTIN LUTHER KING JR. (U.S.A.)

Born:	Died:	Age:
15 January 1929	4 April 1968	39

"A man who won't die for something is not fit to live."

~ Martin Luther King Jr.

(From "The Words Of Martin Luther King, Jr.")

FAISAL IBN ABDUL AZIZ

Saudi Arabia is the only country which is named after its ruling family, the House of Saud. The roots of modern day Saudi Arabia began in the early 1900s when Abdul Aziz al-Saud captured the city of Riyadh and surrounding regions from Turkish control.

In 1906, Abdul and his wife, Tarfah, had a son named Faisal, meaning "the sword." At a young age, Faisal's mother died, and as a result, his grandparents were involved in his education and upbringing. Faisal's grandfather Sheikh (pronounced shake) Muhammad ibn Abd al-Wahhab was well known for his knowledge and his oratory skills. Faisal learned the skill of debate from his grandfather, which would benefit him in later years as Faisal persuaded Islamic elders to accept innovation.

This is difficult because orthodox Islamic culture considers innovation to be dangerous.

While growing up with his grandparents in Riyadh, Faisal still saw his father. When his father was in town, he sent for Faisal and his other small children. They would play after dinner. Later, they would go on picnics and travel outside the city.

Faisal became involved in politics at an early age. When he was only 14, Faisal ibn (son of) Abdul Aziz, headed a delegation to Britain, congratulating the Allies on winning World War I. After his return, Faisal assisted his father in reclaiming other territories. As a result, he became viceroy at the age of 21 over the province where Mecca (Makkah) is located. Mecca is one of the holy Islamic cities for the Muslim pilgrimage.

In 1932, Faisal's father took the Arab regions under his control and formed the Kingdom of Saudi Arabia. Instead of a constitution, the monarchy is based on Islamic law, also known as Shariah. The nation's flag bears a sword and states in Arabic "There is no god but God, and Muhammad is the messenger of God."

It was custom and legal for men to have up to four wives and families at a time in Saudi Arabia. Faisal had already married twice for political reasons.

In 1932, he met a woman named Iffat al-Thunayan. She lived in Turkey for years with her mother. The mother had asked Faisal to help in settling a land dispute in regard to an inheritance from her deceased husband.

Faisal and Iffat married. They grew in love and happiness together. Having lived in Turkey, she was accustomed to more freedom than women normally had in Saudi Arabia.

She influenced Faisal to help provide education for girls. At first they were called clubs to ease in the introduction, but classrooms were built for the first all girls' schools within Saudi Arabia. Girls were not forced to attend but encouraged. Some of the girls progressed onto college, attending with the assistance of scholarships from Iffat.

Striking Oil

After the kingdom is formed, oil is discovered by a company, now known as the Saudi Arabian Oil Company or Saudi Aramco. However, this does not make a serious impact until after World War II ends in 1945. In the last year of the war, Saudi Arabia abandoned its neutral position and declared war against Germany. Although not an active participant in the war, the declaration allowed Saudi Arabia to participate in the founding of the United Nations. Prince Faisal attended the organizational meetings held in San Francisco.

The oil boom started and led to improvements in transportation, including the construction of the Ad-Dammam-Riyadh Railroad and developing Ad Dammam as a deepwater port for oil tankers. Electricity came to many towns. Saudi relied on foreign labor for much of the oil industry, and homes were built to accommodate the increase in population.

In early 1945, King Abdul of Saudi Arabia invited U.S. President Franklin D. Roosevelt to meet at the Suez Canal. Their shipboard meeting demonstrated culture shock. The king's cook wanted to bring 100 live sheep on board. The livestock would be killed to prepare a feast for the dignitaries and all of the crew. The cook explained that the king could not eat food prepared from little metal cans.

The captain allowed the chef to bring seven sheep on board just to prepare the king's meal. There was also concern when the king's crew started open fires to prepare coffee, which happened to be near live ammunition.

After meals were safely prepared, the Saudis found the ship's compass extremely useful. It helped point the way toward Mecca. Saudis pray five times a day while facing Mecca.

The American president, the Saudi king and his son Prince Faisal discussed Palestine and the Jewish population who had survived the concentration camps.

President Roosevelt asked King Abdul about the international community helping the Jewish survivors with a homeland. The king's response was:

"Give them the choicest lands of the Germans." This was reported in the book "Faisal" by Rebecca Stefoff.

Palestine / Israel

The territory sometimes known as Palestine and sometimes known as Israel has been an area in conflict for several millenniums. In biblical times, the Jewish population was viewed as the chosen ones in the Christian faith and inhabited the land of Israel after a hard fought journey to make it to what was called the Promised Land.

In A.D. 135, Jewish settlers were expelled by the Romans. The land became occupied by

Palestinians who were primarily Muslim. In the 1800s, Jewish immigrants started coming to Palestine. They were fleeing persecution and anti-Semitic behavior in Europe. At that time, the territory was not overpopulated. The Ottoman Turks controlled the region and viewed the Jewish population as helping to develop the area.

To all of those of Jewish, Muslim and Christian faith, this area holds extreme religious significance.

During World War I, Britain conquered the Ottoman's hold on the Middle East territory. Britain advised Arab leaders that this area would be given independence. Britain also promised the Zionist leaders that a Jewish homeland would be created in Palestine. This was viewed as conflicting promises.

During World War II, when Adolf Hitler and the Nazi Party tried to commit genocide on the Jewish population, it became more pressing for them to have their own country.

Before the creation of the country, Faisal had spoken on behalf of the Arab nations that this land remain for the Palestinians as their home. When traveling to the United Nations (U.N.) meeting in New York, Zionist demonstrators booed and spat at Faisal as he entered the U.N. building.

After the country of Israel was created in May 1948, then U.S. President Harry Truman recognized the new nation the same day it was formed.

Return To The Desert

In 1953, Faisal's father knew he needed an heir to the throne. He had Faisal and Faisal's half brother Saud brought to him. It was King Abdul's command that after his death, Saud would become king and the younger Faisal would be crown prince, meaning next in line for the throne. King Abdul died on 9 November 1953, and his instructions were followed.

After the king's death, his body was returned to the desert. In the tradition of the Wahhabi, the body is buried in the sand. One rock marks the head of the grave and another rock marks the foot. No inscriptions are placed on the grave markers due to tradition. The body becomes one with the desert.

Financial Crisis

In the early part of the 1950s, Saudi Arabia experienced more income as a result of oil. By 1956, spending had increased beyond the extra income.

The debt continued to grow; soldiers and civil servants had not been paid for months.

Capital left the country until the treasury was empty and the kingdom bankrupt. King Saud retained his title during this time; however, Prince Faisal received the responsibility of restoring the finances. Budgets were created, even for the royal family, where members received a monthly stipend.

Other measures included obtaining short-term loans to cover obligations. Building projects were placed on hold until more funds were available.

In the late 1950s and early 1960s, King Saud relinquished executive power to Prince Faisal during difficult times.

Broadcasting

In January 1964, the Saudi government entered into an agreement with the National Broadcasting Company (NBC) in New York to create a television network. On 17 July 1965, transmissions began from the capital in Riyadh and from the city of Jeddah.

Television and radio systems were developed to build national unity, to modernize communications and to enhance the image of Saudi Arabia abroad. An extreme Muslim group launched an armed attack against the Riyadh television station when it opened. One of the leaders was a Saudi prince, who was killed in the clash with police.

To help the people accept the new technology, religious programming became an important part of broadcasting to show its value to religious authorities.

King Saud's Exile

In 1964, members of the royal family with the support of religious leaders decided to oust King Saud from the throne. While Prince Faisal was on a retreat, the family decided he would officially be king.

While in exile, Saud moved to several places. He lived in Beirut, Lebanon; Cairo, Egypt; Athens, Greece and then the Greek islands. Suffering from ill health, he died in February 1969.

King Faisal's Reign

In 1964, King Faisal officially became the head of the monarchy. He was already well versed in compromise. He had enabled broadcasting to be developed in Saudi Arabia but had not allowed going to see the movies at a cinema. Television it was felt helped to promote family life because people stayed home.

King Faisal started each day at dawn where he would kneel in the courtyard for the first prayer of the day to Allah. Often, there would be guests staying at his private palace. From 9 to 10 a.m., he would be at the government palace, where visitors were received in council chambers.

While there, he worked in his government office. Then, it was back to the private palace for his midday prayer. Lunch would be held with advisers and / or guests.

After lunch and a short rest, it was time for the afternoon prayer and then return to the office.

Around sunset, he went to the desert to meet male relatives for evening prayers. Dinner would be held back at the private palace with guests. Around 9 p.m., he returned to the government office to work until approximately 11:30 p.m. Then at midnight, his advisers and other governmental leaders discussed issues. This time was also used to listen to radio broadcasts.

As a result of his travels abroad, King Faisal knew that Saudi Arabia had to be part of the international community to have a place in the modern world.

His vision was to make the most of the oil wealth to benefit all of the people. He wanted the country to become more independent from foreign governments and also from the oil companies.

King Faisal began long-range economic and social welfare programs for his subjects. He also provided moral and financial support to other Arab countries in the Middle East.

He once stated that "like it or not, we must join the modern world and find an honorable place in it," (from "King Faisal and the Modernization of Saudi Arabia)."

Oil As A Weapon

King Faisal realized that oil represented not just financial power but political power as well. He put this to the test in 1973. He publicly stated that Saudi Arabia would decrease oil supply if the United States government (then under President Richard Nixon) did not change its support for Israel.

On 16 October 1973, all of the Arab countries except for Iran agreed to raise the price of crude oil by 70 percent (from U.S. $1.77 a barrel to U.S. $3.05 per barrel). Before it was over, the price would increase 400 percent in a matter of months.

The Organization of Petroleum Exporting Countries (OPEC) met on 17 October 1973 and voted to reduce oil production by five percent from the previous month.

Unless the Israeli military withdrew from Arab lands, the cutback would increase an additional five percent each month. In the United States, President Nixon asked Congress to approve $2.2 billion to Israel for emergency military aid.

After this announcement, the Arab nations banded together and instituted an embargo on all exports from the United States. As a result of events, some service stations in the United States ran out of gas. At others, the line might last for hours before reaching the gas pump. The crisis was the worst experienced since World War II for the United States, Canada, Japan and Europe.

The embargo ended after five months as part of the negotiations at the Washington Oil Summit.

Saudi's First Development Plan

The First Development Plan occurred between 1970 and 1975 and included the following advances. The government allocated funds on educating Saudi citizens, both at home and abroad. Agricultural land increased substantially and was augmented by irrigation and drainage projects. King Faisal created a Ministry of Justice who was assisted by a Supreme Judicial Council. In addition to administering the laws of Islam, the council examined lower court decisions involving sentences of amputation, stoning or death.

King Faisal's reign became known for far-reaching economic, educational and administrative initiatives. King Faisal's health began to decline. Around 1974, he advised of the fatigue he felt. Similar to his father, he began to have fears that the younger generations were losing their cultural values.

One of the king's nephews had previously gone to college in the United States and not adjusted well. The U.S. State Department intervened on behalf of the Saudi royal family when the college student had allegedly possessed drugs. King Faisal ordered him to remain at home.

The nephew was also the brother of the prince who was killed during the attack on the television station. On 25 March 1975, the nephew came to see King Faisal at work. He shot and killed his uncle – the king. Several months later, the assassin was beheaded with a golden sword.

The king's body was taken and placed in a humble grave outside of Riyadh. As with his father, no inscribed stone was placed on the grave.

Four years later, in honor of his memory, the King Faisal Foundation was created. One of its philanthropic activities includes an annual award. The King Faisal International Prize recognizes individuals who have dedicated their lives to serving others. A prize can be awarded in any of these categories: Arabic literature, Islamic studies, mathematics, medicine or service to Islam.

For 11 years, Faisal officially served as king, but his legacy will remain for centuries to come. He worked to do what was best for his fellow Muslims.

SUSAN VOLLMER

KING FAISAL (Saudi Arabia)		
Born: (estimated) 17 May 1904/1905/1906	Died: 25 March 1975	Age: 68/69/70

"The important thing about a regime is not what it is called but how it acts. There are corrupt republican regimes and sound monarchies and vice versa. The only true criterion of a regime – whether it be monarchical or republican – is the degree of reciprocity between the ruler and ruled and the extent to which it symbolizes prosperity, progress and healthy initiative."

~King Faisal

(Reported in the book "King Faisal and the Modernization of Saudi Arabia.")

STEPHEN BANTU BIKO

In the 1950s and 1960s in South Africa, the oppressiveness of apartheid enveloped many blacks who formed a silent majority. Apartheid means strict segregation of people based on race.

One person whose life was dedicated to the fight against apartheid was Stephen Bantu Biko (pronounced bee kaw). Steve was born on 18 December 1946 in King William's Town, South Africa. His parents appropriately chose the name "Bantu," which means people.

His father, who died when Steve was only four, left behind a wife and four children, including Steve.

Steve started fighting for people's rights while studying medicine in college. As a delegate for an organization called the National Union of South

African Students, Steve participated in an annual conference. During the conference in July 1967 at Rhodes University in Grahamstown, Steve became insulted when he and other black delegates were given accommodations further away at a church hall. At the same time, white student delegates were being placed on-site at the university.

Black Consciousness Movement

Steve began to question the point of liberal groups comprised primarily of white persons. He advocated and formed a group two years later whose membership could only be black and named it the South African Student's Organisation (SASO). The goal was to remove the inferiority complex many blacks had and replace it with a positive social image.

This became known as the Black Consciousness Movement. Steve believed that blacks had to be in leadership positions and that only blacks could push the liberation movement. If white people did this for blacks, then this would reinforce the idea that blacks were not capable of taking control and responsibility for themselves. Steve saw the need to free people from both the physical and mental bonds of oppression.

To help create positive self-awareness in blacks, Steve created night-classes, encouraging education and the development of more skills. He advocated diversity and that each of us has different skills to contribute.

Steve authored a column for a South African student newspaper using the pen name of "Frank Talk." The title of his column was "I Write What I Like." An excerpt from one of his columns on black consciousness and culture reads:

> "No wonder the African child learns to hate his heritage in his days at school. So negative is the image presented to him that he tends to find solace only in close identification with the white society."

> "No doubt, therefore, part of the approach envisaged in bringing about 'Black Consciousness' has to be directed to the past, to seek to rewrite the history of the black man and to produce in it the heroes who form the core of the African background."

Leadership

At the end of the 1960s with political activist Nelson Mandela in prison, Steve served as a new leader. Even though he fathered the Black Consciousness Movement, he viewed that the struggle was shared by many. He thought of himself as one spokesperson addressing the youth of the country toward confidence and dignity.

During meetings, he often sat in the back of the room and listened while others spoke. After discussions finished, the group would look to him for guidance. He was not propelled by bitterness, regarding the issues facing blacks. Instead, he moved forward with integrity and courage, motivating and bringing others into the group.

International Recognition

While Steve opposed apartheid, he also opposed violence. This stance helped him gain international recognition. He challenged U.S. politicians who opposed South Africa's apartheid system but had not taken a strong stance with economic sanctions. The South African government viewed Steve as a threat to its status quo. Word had spread of a possible alliance between Steve's organization and the racially integrated African National Congress (ANC).

Banning

In March 1973, Steve and seven other leaders of the South African Student's Organisation were "banned." Banning meant that they could no longer speak in public, write articles, travel outside the city nor meet with more than one person at a time.

When asked by writer Donald Woods what it was like to be banned, Steve replied:

> "Don't you realize what a ban is? It isn't a preventive measure. It's a way of punishing people the state cannot punish under normal law. Many of the banning restrictions are designed simply to inconvenience or exasperate. At first it doesn't seem too inconvenient to have to report to a police station once a week – but after a year it seems an intolerable inconvenience. Talking to one person at a time is designed to inconvenience you by making you repeat everything you said to the last person to the next

person as well. It is to keep you looking over your shoulder, even in your own home."

(Reported in the book "Biko"
by Donald Woods)

On the evening of 18 August 1977, Steve and a friend, Peter Jones were traveling to Grahamstown, South Africa, in a Peugeot station wagon. His friend was driving when they were stopped by the police at a roadblock. They were taken in for questioning for the distribution of pamphlets and charged under South Africa's Terrorism Act. They stayed in separate cells in a prison near Port Elizabeth with no due process of law nor any contact with a lawyer.

Steve's first 20 days of prison meant being chained to a bedpost while naked. He only left the cell for police interrogations. During one or more of the interrogations, he was severely beaten. On 11 September 1977, a guard found him foaming at the mouth and semiconscious. He was taken to a hospital 700 miles away in Pretoria where he died on 12 September 1977. His friend lived and was later released from prison.

The Aftermath

Steve's death while in police custody brought international condemnation. This led to the United Nations and the United States imposing sanctions against South Africa. At the time of his death, Steve had a wife, Ntsiki; two sons - Nkosinathi and Khaya; plus a daughter, Bandi. In one of his writings, Steve said:

> "I've devoted my life to see equality for blacks, and at the same time, I've denied the needs of my family. Please understand that I take these actions, not out of selfishness or arrogance, but to preserve a South Africa worth living in for blacks and whites."

The Inquest

On 14 November 1977, the local and international press attended the start of the inquest into the death of Steve Biko. Over a three-week period, testimony was given in a courtroom in Pretoria.

The autopsy report stated that extensive brain injury had led to kidney failure and uremia, which means renal failure. This sometimes occurs suddenly as a result of physical trauma or exposure to toxic chemicals.

When one of the guards was questioned why Steve was kept in leg irons, he first replied that the office was not locked. Then, he said it was the custom to use chains. The security police testified that Steve had been kept naked because they thought it would prevent him from committing suicide or from escaping.

When questioned why Steve's family had not been notified of his serious injuries and his transfer to a hospital, a colonel on staff replied he believed that Steve was shamming (just pretending to be seriously injured).

The lawyer representing the Biko family estimated that Steve had been assaulted four or five days before he became semiconscious.

At the end, the magistrate presented his findings to the court:

- The cause of death was a brain injury and other complications.
- Injuries were most likely received in a scuffle with security police.
- Death cannot be contributed to a particular person.

The South African government did not charge anyone with the death of Stephen Bantu Biko.

STEPHEN BANTU BIKO (South Africa)		
Born: 18 December 1946	Died: 12 September 1977	Age: 30
"You are either alive and proud or you are dead, and when you are dead, you can't care anyway. And your method of death can itself be a politicizing thing. ... So if you can overcome the personal fear for death, which is a highly irrational thing, you know, then you're on the way." ~ Steve Bantu Biko (Reported in The New Republic magazine)		

ANWAR EL-SADAT

Anwar el-Sadat became known for the contributions he made in bringing peace to the volatile Middle East in the late 1970s and early 1980s. He was born to a Muslim family on Christmas Day, 25 December 1918; how appropriate for a man who served as a bridge among Muslims, Jews and Christians.

Anwar's family came from a village in Egypt along the Nile Delta named Mit Abul-Kum. His father became the first in the village to graduate from elementary school and received the honor of being referred to as "the educated man." Anwar's father worked as a clerk at an Egyptian military hospital based in the country of Sudan. His mother was the daughter of a freed slave from Sudan.

As his mother's pregnancy advanced, she went back to the Egyptian village to give birth. Her mother-in-law was well respected as the village healer for her knowledge of ancient Arab remedies. The grandmother was also excellent with children. Anwar and three of his siblings were born at his grandmother's home, and they spent part of their childhood being raised by her.

His grandmother supervised the small 2.5 acre farm they had. She sent Anwar to school, however, to obtain an education. First, he went to the Quranic teaching school to learn Arabic reading and writing and also to memorize the Quran. His next school was the Coptic Christian school.

In 1925, at the age of six or seven, Anwar and the entire family moved to Cairo. His parents, grandmother and siblings lived in a four-room family flat. Later, his father added a second wife, which is common in Arabic culture. The second wife had nine children, and they all lived in the same four-room family flat.

Anwar still remembered a family named Afifi from the village, where he grew up, playing with the other children. He asked Eqbal Afifi to marry him, but her family initially disapproved due to his lower social status.

In 1936, Egypt remained under British dominance when a military school opened. For the first time, those of other social classes could be considered to be an officer in the Egyptian Army. The military provided an escape from poverty. Anwar was among the first students to attend. Upon graduation from the academy in 1938, the Afifi family finally gave permission for Anwar to marry their daughter. The wedding took place two years later. After the academy, Anwar went to a remote military outpost where he met a man named Gamal Abdel Nasser. Gamal, Anwar and some other revolutionaries established the Free Officers Movement in 1939, whose main purpose was the overthrow of British rule and the current Egyptian monarchy. As a result of Anwar's activities within the group, he was imprisoned twice.

Life In Prison

During his first stay in prison, Anwar had a comfortable cell with a small table, bed and blanket. He asked for and received newspapers and books, which helped improve his English skills.

He was relocated to several different detention centers, and at one, he met a German prisoner who taught him how to speak and read in German.

He would later escape from prison. While living as a fugitive in Egypt, Anwar received a reprieve because Britain dropped the martial laws, which had previously been used to imprison him.

His next arrest involved being a conspirator in an assassination of a public official. The official was considered a traitor by the Free Officers.

At the same time, one of Anwar's young daughters died while he was in prison. She developed a fever, and there was no money for medicine nor proper nutrition. Then, during the summer of 1946, while Anwar was still in prison, his wife gave birth to another child. She was called Rawia, the same name as the child who had died.

This prison was much harsher than the detention camps of the past. He was held in solitary confinement. Instead of furniture, he had a mat, which was on the floor and a dirty blanket. There was no radio or companionship. Instead, he meditated. He prayed. He came to know his true self in the dark confines of a prison cell.

He decided that he had grown apart from his wife. He felt his destiny was that of public service and did not feel she would be able to cope. He was planning to request a divorce. In the meantime, he asked her to stop visiting him in jail.

Anwar's case came to trial and was carried in the newspapers with his photograph. The trial lasted for eight months and concluded in July 1948. The verdict was not guilty.

Jehan (Jean) Safwat Raouf

After his release from prison, Anwar moved out on his own. A long-time friend, Hassan Issat, invited Anwar to come and stay in his home in a city called Suez.

As it turned out, his friend wanted Anwar to assist in some business dealings, which involved the Saudis. After the deal concluded, Anwar felt he was not paid what Hassan originally promised and decided to pursue another job.

Although he was unsatisfied in his business experiences, he was more than pleased at meeting and getting to know another house guest named Jehan. She was the cousin of his friend's wife. Her father was Egyptian and her mother British. She inherited her mother's light complexion and had beautiful dark hair from her father. To her Egyptian friends, she was Jehan. To the British and her parents, she was Jean.

Although she was half-British, Jehan viewed herself as a patriot to Egypt, her homeland. Jehan was already up at 2 a.m. helping prepare a predawn meal during Ramadan. They would eat before the fasting began during the daylight hours.

Hassan brought Anwar to his home. Anwar was sitting in the hallway, while Hassan announced the news in the kitchen that Anwar would be staying there.

Later in her autobiography, Jehan said she saw him in the hallway where he slowly turned to look at her. She recognized his face from the newspaper photographs.

"I knew I should drop my eyes, not look at this man – or any man, for that matter – in a bold manner, but at the moment I had no control."

His eyes looked solemn and sad, and he appeared to carry the burdens of the world. She felt the weariness he was carrying. They shook hands but said nothing.

The family and Anwar sat down for the predawn meal. He ate very little and did not say anything. He did not speak for two days.

Jehan thought he seemed mysterious. She found out later that this was his way of thinking over decisions he needed to make by meditating and contemplating in silence.

One day, she brought him a fig from the garden. He smiled and asked if she had just celebrated a birthday. She had. She invited him on the family trip that day to the beach along the Red Sea. Jehan loved to sing in the car and did so most of the way. At one point though, Anwar suddenly announced he could not buy anything for her birthday, but he would sing a song. Instead of looking somber, his face came alive as he sang a song of love in a beautiful voice while looking at Jehan.

After the family had lunch, Jehan and Anwar walked along the beach talking for several hours. Jehan asked many questions, and Anwar seemed relieve to speak of his time in prison and of his first family. While in prison, Anwar could not provide for his family. His father had helped with what he could, and an organization called the Muslim Brotherhood sent 10 pounds every month to his wife for her and the children.

His first wife was a distant cousin. Their marriage was to help solidify the family and the land. He felt a duty toward his first wife, and he felt pain at the suffering he was causing. "How could I punish my wife with divorce when she has done nothing but wait for me all these years?"

Jehan wrote later in her autobiography that the Quran states, "Among lawful things, the one that God hates most is divorce."

For a year and a half in prison, Anwar contemplated his marriage. His temples throbbed when he went to sleep at night and still throbbed when he awoke in the morning.

After Jehan's and Anwar's walk along the beach, they returned to her relatives. Anwar questioned the cousin several times about Jehan's age. She had just turned 15, and Anwar was 30. On another occasion, they were all out celebrating the end of Ramadan. She confided in her cousin that she was falling in love with Anwar. The cousin counseled Jehan to be careful but also offered to sit with them so they could be together more. They were in essence having a courtship, which was unheard of at that time in Egypt.

Jehan already had several potential suitors trying to obtain her hand for marriage. To her, they all paled in comparison to Anwar. She felt they were not meant for her.

She loved Anwar despite the differences in their ages, his questionable employment future and his financial commitments to his first family.

She wanted to marry him but could not without her parents' consent. Her respect for them and for what she believed in the Quran required it. She returned to her parents' home in Cairo. Her cousin's husband, Hassan, at first pleaded the case for Jehan's benefit but to no avail.

Her father had married for love against the wishes of his parents. He finally agreed with Jehan, but they still had to convince her mother. Jehan's mother then said she would at least meet Anwar.

During their meeting, her mom grilled Anwar while Jehan and her father remained silent. She asked about the British occupation of Egypt, which Anwar confirmed he still opposed. She asked if he wanted to see all of the British people leave Egypt, which he did not.

A second meeting was set up. Jehan advised Anwar in advance to discuss books because her mother loved to read. Anwar discussed the novels of the English writer Charles Dickens. Anwar enjoyed "Great Expectations" and "Oliver Twist." These Dickens' novels focused on orphans. In the Quran, it says to be kind and fair to orphans. At the age of six, the prophet Muhammad had become an orphan. A child is considered orphaned in this culture, even if only one parent dies.

Jehan's mother finally gave her approval. They became engaged, and the wedding day came on 29 May 1949. In Egyptian custom, it was fine for the groom to see the bride before the wedding.

Jehan's nanny performed the first ceremony of the wedding day called the halawa. By using a heated mixture of lemons and sugar, this process (similar to waxing in the west) removes the hair from the legs and arms of a woman. Jehan felt clean and ready after the halawa. She dressed and waited for Anwar to take her to the dressmaker.

Anwar came to her house in his full military uniform. It was illegal for him to wear it because the British had dismissed him from the army. (Fortunately, he was not arrested on their wedding day.)

Jehan put on the wedding dress and veil. Then, the dressmaker applied makeup, which Jehan had never worn before. The next stop was the photographer, who remarked that she was one of the loveliest brides he had ever seen. The portrait showed the military officer and his bride with the flowing veil, draped across the floor. Next to the veil was a bouquet of flowers.

At Egyptian weddings, the bride must be at least 21 to enter into a legal contract of marriage.

When she is not, the dad steps in. So due to Jehan's age, her father took her place and held hands with Anwar. A white handkerchief was placed over their hands when the sheik performed the Muslim marriage ceremony.

She sat in the same room with the family, so she could watch the marriage proceedings. In some cases, the bride and her bridesmaids are placed in a separate room during the ceremony.

When the sheik asked Jehan's father if he approved of the union, he looked at Jehan for confirmation. She vigorously nodded yes, almost dislodging her veil.

The reception party at her aunt's house lasted all night long. They had three dancing horses with flowers braided into their manes and tails. They did pirouettes to the sound of a single flute.

In addition to the horses, other entertainment included singers, belly dancers, musicians and a comedian.

She and Anwar sat on two wedding thrones decorated with flowers. They watched the festivities throughout the early morning hours and ate from the elaborate buffet.

They had known in advance that their apartment was not finished yet. It was located in a new building that was not yet ready.

Jehan and Anwar left the wedding reception for a drive out to see the pyramids. They walked over the sand and looked up at the nearly 500-foot Great Pyramid. They watched the sun rise, admiring the dawn of the desert.

Jehan would later write:

"Never have I felt so full of hope, for my husband, for my country, for all the riches and wonders of Egypt that had gone before, for all the promise that lay ahead."

As the sun went higher in the sky, Anwar returned Jehan to her family's home, and he returned to the boardinghouse where he had been staying.

Return To The Military

While Anwar had been in prison, Gamal Nasser had continued to grow the Free Officers Movement. With Anwar out of prison and a not guilty verdict from the trial, he was able to be re-installed in the Egyptian Army in 1950.

In late 1951, the Free Officers started making plans to stage a coup and take over the government in 1955. However, Gamal decided to move the timetable up. One factor was an event called Black Saturday. Young Egyptians rioted for the British to leave the Suez Canal Zone.

The British who viewed the Suez Canal as belonging to Great Britain started searching Egyptians who were in the area. This increased the number of riots culminating on 25 January 1952. British soldiers killed 70 Egyptian police officers.

Afterward, an angry mob committed arson burning down a bank, bars, cafes and movie theaters. A shop with firearms was broken into and looted. Black Saturday convinced them to move the revolution up to November 1952.

A second factor in the decision was when Gamal found out the identity of some of the Free Officers had been compromised, so the revolution was moved up even more to July of the same year.

The Free Officers entered the army headquarters. Two soldiers were killed defending it. The Free Officers took control of the headquarters, the other government buildings and the radio station. The British-controlled Egyptian king remained on the throne. He was asked to leave the country by 26

July 1952. The king sailed to Europe and went into exile.

Anwar oversaw the official abdication of the king. Gamal would later take charge as president with Anwar as his most trusted lieutenant.

Suez Crisis

When Anwar was growing up, his grandmother told him stories about the Suez Canal in Egypt. A French company began digging the canal in 1859 with Egyptian labor. Egyptians used picks and shovels to dig a 100-mile trench in the desert.

The intent was to create a waterway where European ships could go from the Mediterranean Sea to the Red Sea without sailing around the vast African continent.

While digging the canal, many Egyptians died of hunger and disease. The canal finished in 1869. After completion, the new waterway did not benefit Egyptians. Egypt had a foreign ruler at the time who sold the shares to Britain when Egypt faced bankruptcy in 1875.

Now in 1956 with Gamal as president, he decided to claim the Suez Canal as rightfully belonging to Egypt. The country would take over the ownership and operation.

Egyptian Army squads moved into the canal offices. Britain and France who had controlled the canal called up troops.

At first, Britain and France would not pay the tolls for international passage. Gamal let the ships pass. Then, the majority of the British and French canal ship pilots walked off the job.

Egyptian pilots then navigated the ocean ships through, except for Israeli ships which were barred from access. Israel sent troops out to the canal while Britain and France bombed Egyptian air bases.

From 29 October through 4 November 1956, the Suez War lasted seven days. During the height of the battle, Egypt asked Russia for help which was denied. At this point, Anwar thought it was best not to depend on the Russians again.

Egypt also asked U.S. President Dwight Eisenhower for assistance. The United States pressured the allies to withdraw and leave Egypt controlling the canal, which did happen. This impressed Anwar.

Six-Day War (5 June 1967—10 June 1967)

In 1960, Anwar suffered a heart attack. He recovered and his friendship with Gamal strengthened. Gamal advised the Egyptian council that the Arab world was criticizing Egypt for allowing Israeli ships through the Strait of Tiran. However, if Egypt closed the passage, this would result in war.

On 2 June 1967, the entire council including Anwar voted to close the strait to Israel. On 5 June 1967, the Six-Day War began. The Israeli troops attacked Egyptian air bases while the Egyptian commander-in-chief of the armed forces was doing an aerial inspection of his troops. He had ordered all Egyptian anti-aircraft guns to hold fire while he did his inspection.

During this time the Israelis attacked, destroying all of the aircraft on the ground. Israel's troops became victors and captured Golan Heights from Syria, the West Bank from Jordan and the Gaza Strip and Sinai Peninsula up to the Suez Canal.

It was a crushing blow for Egypt and its citizens. The government broke off diplomatic relations with the United States.

A President Dies

In 1969, President Gamal Nasser appointed Anwar as vice president of his administration. Egypt and the Arab countries still felt humiliated by the Six-Day War. In one of his memoirs, Anwar wrote:

> "We in Egypt suffered the most pain, grief and bitterness. The largest and most powerful of the Arab states, we had suffered the greatest disaster in our history, ancient or modern."

Egypt felt mocked because the country had not defeated Israel, a country whose population was smaller than a medium-sized Arab city. Relations continued to deteriorate also between Egypt and the United States.

On 28 September 1970, U.S. President Richard Nixon was in the Mediterranean visiting a U.S. naval fleet near the coast of Egypt. The visit served as a reminder of the U.S. force in that area. While President Nixon was with the U.S. fleet, he received a message that Egyptian President Gamal Nasser had died.

Anwar appeared on national television to make the official announcement about 11 p.m. that same day that President Gamal Nasser had suffered a fatal heart attack. The U.S. ship canceled the maneuvers, which had been planned. Instead, President Nixon flew early to the next stop on his agenda to visit the president of Yugoslavia. This prevented the Yugoslavian president from attending President Nasser's funeral, much to Anwar's disappointment.

Instead of automatically assuming the Egyptian presidency, Anwar called for a special election. It was held, and he was elected president on 15 October 1970.

The following year, Anwar declared 1971 as the "Year of Decision." He intended for Egypt to reclaim the Sinai which Israel had captured in the Six-Day War. Anwar announced Egypt's intention to have the Sinai back, whether through war or negotiation.

Yom Kippur War (6 October 1973 – 24 October 1973)

Anwar made preparations for war at the same time he sought an acceptable Middle East plan via the United States. He felt that he was not getting the U.S. support he needed.

He contemplated what the most destructive weapon was and came to the conclusion that it was oil. He obtained support from King Faisal of Saudi Arabia, the largest oil producer in the Middle East. Those who supported Israel would be deprived of oil, resulting in a worldwide crisis.

On 6 October 1973, Anwar selected Yom Kippur as the attack day. It was the holiest day of the Jewish year when there would be much fasting and prayers in synagogues. October was also one of the better months for crossing the tides in the canal.

At 2 p.m. on 6 October with the sun in the eyes of the Israelis, Egypt flew 222 jets across the canal and fired 3,000 guns.

High-pressure water pumps, such as those used for fighting fires, washed away the Israeli sand walls.

Both sides needed more ammunition and equipment and sent appeals for help. The Soviets sent supplies to Egyptian and Syrian airports. The U.S. sent supply planes to Israel. When Anwar asked President Josip Broz Tito of Yugoslavia to send 100 tanks, he sent 140 with full tanks of fuel and ammunition.

Anwar's wife, Jehan, visited hospitals, caring for the wounded. She rolled bandages for the Egyptian Red Crescent Society, part of the Red Cross.

On 22 October 1973, the United Nations Security Council declared a cease fire. Anwar was ready to accept it. The war was something of a stand off. Israel recovered its initial loss of territory. However, Egyptians had regained face and proven that Israel could be invaded.

In the following years, Egypt and Israel participated in what was called "shuttle diplomacy" with U.S. Secretary of State Henry Kissinger traveling between the key players to try and work out an agreement on disengagement.

In 1975, Anwar led the convoy that re-opened the Suez Canal. After the canal was re-opened, Israel in a sign of good faith pulled half of its tanks back 20 miles. Egypt and Israel signed a second disengagement agreement.

Food Riots

For a long period, Egypt has suffered from overpopulation with the majority of the people living on about five percent of the country's land near the Nile River and other waterways. The rest of the country remains a vast desert.

Egypt could not grow enough food to sustain its population. Due to the amount of food that has to be imported, the government had subsidized prices for years to keep basic foods affordable.

In January 1977, the country was in bad financial shape. Anwar's economic advisers suggested reducing the amount of the subsidies. Prices increased dramatically on flour, rice, oil and sugar. Riots began when protesters took to the streets. They smashed windows and set buses on fire. More than a 1,000 people were arrested. Others were killed or injured. Riots began in Alexandria and then spread to Cairo.

Anwar knew that Egyptians were tired of making sacrifices and restored the pricing to where it used to be. He was dismayed at how the riots seemed personally addressed to him, and he realized how much his popularity had diminished with his own people.

With the riots stopped, Anwar knew more needed to be done with the relationship with Israel and to improve his country's finances. The United States had a new president whose name was Jimmy Carter. Anwar went to meet him and trusted him.

The Peace Initiative

In February 1977, U.S. President Jimmy Carter and Egyptian President Anwar el-Sadat started talks on the Arab-Israeli conflict. The agenda included:

- The Arab lands occupied since the Six-Day War in 1967
- The relationship between Arabs and Israelis
- The Palestinian people

President Carter was the first American president to support a homeland for the Palestinian people. Anwar understood why the Zionists, who were Jewish, didn't like President Carter. But, he couldn't understand why other Arab nations didn't support him.

In November of this same year, Anwar announced he would make a journey to Jerusalem. No Arab leader had ever entered into direct negotiations with Israel before.

His plane landed in Tel Aviv on 19 November 1977. There was a long receiving line and international camera crews awaiting his arrival. He shook hands with former prime ministers Golda Meir and Yitzhak Rabin. Israeli citizens lined the streets with Egyptian and Israeli flags and signs in Arabic welcoming him to Israel. He was overwhelmed by the reception he received.

Menachem Begin, Israel's prime minister in 1977, had promised Anwar that he would be welcomed with all of the hospitality that Egyptians and Israelis share from their common father Abraham. And that did happen.

In his speech to the Knesset (Israel's parliament), Anwar stated, "Seventy-five percent of the problem between Israelis and the Arabs is the psychological barrier that divides them."

When Anwar returned home, Egyptians welcomed him and the idea of peace. Western countries viewed him as a statesman and a courageous leader. Arab countries outside of Egypt viewed him as a traitor.

Camp David Accords

U.S. President Jimmy Carter invited Anwar and Menachem Begin to come to Camp David for a summit conference. Camp David is a presidential retreat located about 70 miles (112 kilometers) from Washington, D.C., in the Maryland mountains.

The talks were held 5 through 17 September 1978. Carter smiled as he greeted his guests. They were all religious men – one Jewish, one Muslim and one Christian – but they had a unified purpose of peace in the Middle East.

On the 13th day, a consensus was reached:

- Israel would return the Sinai to Egypt in three stages.
- Egypt would establish diplomatic relations after the first withdrawal.
- Negotiations would be held over a five-year period among Egypt, Israel, Jordan and the Palestinians regarding Gaza and the West Bank.

While Anwar received a warm welcome from Egyptians upon his return, several ministers resigned in protest. Arab leaders met in Iraq and offered Anwar $5 billion dollars to reject the peace accords. Anwar refused.

Anwar and Menachem both received the Nobel Peace Prize in 1978. Menachem accepted his in person in Norway. Anwar did not attend because the peace was not in place yet.

He did donate the proceeds of the Nobel Peace Prize to his hometown village of Mit Abul-Kum. He started planning to retire there and began building a home overlooking the Nile delta.

The peace treaty, which started at Camp David, was finally signed on 26 March 1979 on the White House lawn by Anwar, Menachem and Jimmy Carter.

State Of Emergency

Anwar seemed to be losing control with his own people and was also less patient in weathering political storms. When the Egyptian Parliament voted on the Camp David Accords, Anwar did not consider the approval large enough. He dissolved parliament and demanded new elections. More than 60 persons who had criticized the Camp David Accords were arrested, including former members of parliament.

On 6 October 1981, Anwar put on a new uniform to attend the military parade in Nasser City commemorating the Yom Kippur War. He sat across from the Tomb of the Unknown Soldier with his vice president and minister of defense. The air show started just before 1 p.m. as everyone admired the aircraft overhead. At the same time, a truck pulled up with Egyptian terrorists. Anwar stood up and was fatally shot. He had been killed by Muslim fundamentalists.

Despite the leader's assassination, Israel abided by the previously agreed to peace treaty and finished its withdrawal from the Sinai in the following year after Anwar's death.

In a tribute to Anwar, U.S. Secretary of State Kissinger said, "Peace will be his pyramid."

ANWAR EL-SADAT (Egypt)		
Born: 25 December 1918	Died: 6 October 1981	Age: 62

"This is my fate. No man can escape his fate. The day of my death is set beforehand by God. It might take place in Jerusalem or in Cairo, on a bridge or under a bridge. The hour is coming, have no doubt. How can we forget the words of God almighty: 'Wherever you may be, death shall overtake you; even though you be in fortified castles.' "

~ Anwar el-Sadat

(From his book "Those I Have Known")

INDIRA (NEHRU) GANDHI

For more than a 100 years, Britain dominated a country of vast size and population known as India. One name frequently associated with India is Gandhi. This name commonly found in India means "grocer." Some of the famous Gandhis were like grocers, feeding the people of India ideas and hopes of a self-reliant, independent country.

Born on 19 November 1917, Indira was the only child for her parents, Jawaharlal and Kamala Nehru. Her birth took place in the family mansion named Anand Bhavan, when translated from Hindi means "House Of Happiness."

Her grandfather as head of the household named her Indira after his own mother. Her nickname while growing up became Indu, which means "moon child."

As one of the most successful lawyers in the area, her grandfather had the first home in Allahabad (now known as Prayagraj) with running water and electricity. The House of Happiness had gardens, a lawn for croquet, a tennis court and an indoor swimming pool. The 42-room mansion had many furnishings, which had been imported from Britain.

Her father and grandfather met a well-known pacifist named Mahatma Gandhi. Mahatma helped convince them to support the anti-colonial movement for freedom from Britain.

One of Mahatma's ideas was for the Indians to show how strongly they felt about independence from Britain by burning all of their British-made goods. A huge pile of clothing made of silks, satins and velvets was thrown on the family lawn. The bonfire was set to symbolize an India free of foreign control.

Indu had learned that nothing was as important as the struggle for independence.

Civil Disobedience

India fought a different type of war with the British. Instead of using rifles and ammunition, they armed themselves with a mindset called civil disobedience.

The Indians did not recognize the laws of the English, especially those they felt were wrong. They did not pay taxes. Not only had they burned items "made in England," they also started a boycott. This meant they would not buy items which were made in England and imported to India.

Participating in civil disobedience resulted in conflicts with the police. Her grandmother had even been beaten with a nightstick by a police officer. One day, when Indu was about four years old, her mother took her to her first trial. Indu sat next to her grandfather who was on trial but offered no defense regarding the charge that he belonged to a political group – the Congress Party. Her grandfather was sentenced to six months in jail and fined to pay 500 Indian rupees.

Her father was in a different court on that same day. He was accused of distributing leaflets encouraging the boycott of English merchants. He received the same sentence as his father.

The family would not pay the English court fines. As a result, the government sent police over to the mansion to remove family treasures of artwork and jewelry as payment.

With both her father and grandfather in jail, she realized the significance of what they were fighting for. She would even announce to the servants at home that they should do their part and be arrested, too!

There was even a time when the police arrested her mother, Kamala. The House of Happiness had grown more quiet. Indu spent much time in the family library with their books and her love of reading.

Indira adjusted to the instability of her home life. She related to fighting for freedom. Spying on the police was a game she and her friends played.

Monkey Brigade

When Indu tried to join the Congress Party, she was told she was too young. So, she decided to start her own group of children to help in the struggle for independence. The name she created was the "Monkey Brigade." Based on a classic Indian story, a group of monkeys formed a bridge, which helped the hero reach his wife and rescue her from the evil captors.

An estimated 1,000 to 2,000 children participated in the brigade. They delivered messages for the adults, they brought food and drinks to rallies, they hung flags and they even spied on police.

While playing near officers, they would report back any conversations overhead. One of the members of the Monkey Brigade was Feroze Gandhi, who was no relation to Mahatma.

Indu's grandfather had a new and smaller home built for the family. He did not have as much income anymore to support the large home because of money given away to help others and items taken by the police in lieu of fines. The smaller place would still be called the House of Happiness.

Education

Indu's education was not always traditional. They learned from Mahatma Gandhi to share possessions with the less fortunate, especially those suffering from leprosy.

Due to numerous prison terms at different times, her father ended up spending about nine years in prison when added together. He compensated for these absences by writing letters to Indu, teaching her about various cultures and countries.

By the time she was 13 years old, Indu had already been in six different schools. Indu's mother had been ill. In the mid-1920s, she was diagnosed with tuberculosis. It was decided she would go to

Switzerland for treatment and live in the fresh mountain air.

One of the schools she attended was called L'Ecole Internationale in Geneva. She learned first hand about different cultures and traditions. An estimated 75 nationalities attended the schools.

In 1927, her mother became well enough to return to India. Two years later, her father became president of the Indian National Congress Party, following in his father's footsteps.

Indu's grandfather died in February 1931 following a short illness. Her mother eventually died from tuberculosis on 28 February 1936 at the age of 36.

Feroze Gandhi

Feroze Gandhi had visited Indira and her mother when she was alive and they were living in Europe. Later, Indira and Feroze would see each other more when they both attended college in Europe. They each shared the experience of being foreign students, yet were still concerned about India's struggle for independence.

Indira and Feroze fell in love. Back in India, she told her father of their plans to marry. He was not pleased. Most marriages in India were arranged by the parents.

Feroze was a Parsee, which refers to a group of ancestors who escaped from Persia (now Iran) centuries earlier. He was considered by society to be from a lower class group, and Indira was criticized for her decision to marry him.

Indira's father relented and gave his blessing for the marriage. On 26 March 1942, Indira and Feroze married on the grounds of the House of Happiness. The traditional Hindu ceremony included taking seven steps around a sacred fire. At the beginning of the ceremony, she sat next to her father. By the end, she sat next to her husband.

Later that year, Indira understood literally what it meant to be in prison. In September 1942, she spoke at a rally and was arrested for supporting civil disobedience. She discovered that being in prison was much worse than visiting one. Zareer Masani quoted her in the book "Indira Gandhi: A Biography" as follows:

> "I had visited jails either for trials of relations and friends or for unsatisfactory but highly treasured 20-minute interviews. . . . What a world of difference there is between hearing and

seeing from the outside and the actual experience. Herded like animals, devoid of dignity or privacy, we were debarred not only from outside company or news but from all beauty and colour, softness and grace."

Indira and Feroze, who had been arrested at the same event for coming to her aid, were both released about August 1943. Indira then focused on motherhood giving birth a year later to their first son, Rajiv, on 20 August 1944. Their second son, who they named Sanjay, was born on 14 December 1946.

Independence

During World War II, England declared war on Nazi Germany. As a result, the British colony of India was also at war with Germany. The Indian National Congress offered to help the British fight Germany if it resulted in freeing India from British rule.

About seven months after the war ended in Europe, England agreed to free India. Indira's father was asked to form a cabinet of ministers who would rule until formal elections were conducted.

In 1946, a movement began to divide India into a Hindu country which would still be called India plus a Muslim country to be named Pakistan. Violence began over the disputes. The British established borders for an East Pakistan and a West Pakistan with India in the center. A mass migration began as Muslims moved into Pakistan and Hindus into India.

In August 1947, India began its self-rule and independence with Indira's father as the country's first prime minister.

A Divided House

When Indira's father was about 60 years of age, he lived alone and needed more assistance. Indira helped him set up his home called Teen Murti which translated stands for "House With Three Statues."

She traveled between her home with Feroze in Lucknow and her home with her father in Delhi. Her father had numerous official state functions where he relied on her to be the hostess.

Feroze became elected to congress in 1952 and moved near his father-in-law's home. When they all had meals together, Indira's father and husband disagreed on nearly every topic.

In 1955, Indira became a member of the working committee for the Congress Party. And four years later, the Congress Party elected her as president. Both her father and grandfather had served in this role. Now, it was her turn. Indira focused on international relations. She encouraged the congress to oppose colonial movements in any country. The Indian Government condemned the racism in South Africa.

In the late 1950s, Feroze suffered a heart attack. He recovered, and they took a vacation in Kashmir, the mountainous region where they had spent their honeymoon.

On 8 September 1960, Feroze died as a result of a massive heart attack. Ironically, her husband's heart had given out while she worked to take care of her father and her country.

Four years later, her father died from a stroke, after serving 17 years in office. Lal Bahadur Shastri became prime minister. During his term, Indira served as minister of information and broadcasting. She liberalized censorship policies, increased the number of hours for broadcasting time and approved a television project to provide education on family planning.

When the prime minister died suddenly of a heart attack in 1966, Indira succeeded him. She then retained the position when an election was held the following year. Indira was officially the first female to head the world's largest democracy.

Indira – The Prime Minister

Indira's schedule as prime minister included waking up around 6 in the morning. She performed her yoga exercises and then quickly groomed for the day's activities.

During breakfast, she looked at newspapers, identifying any relevant items. Around 8:30 a.m., she held morning office hours for colleagues, state leaders, the general public and any other visitors. She was direct in her meetings with people and her leadership style, not wasting time on preliminary small talk.

After lunch, she rested for an hour. Then, based on the day, there could be a cabinet meeting, foreign dignitary visit or administrative work. Evenings were spent discussing political party issues or attending an official banquet. Otherwise, she dined at home and then reviewed files, going to bed around midnight.

Bangladesh

East and West Pakistan broke into a civil war in 1971. At first, she viewed it as an internal problem for Pakistan. Then, she realized that India was becoming the new home for refugees. Approximately 30,000 refugees a day were crossing the border.

Indira did not want to become part of a military confrontation. And she did not want to seal the border either because she felt that was not only inhumane but geographically impossible. An estimated 10 million refugees entered the country of India.

Indira contacted other heads of state to bring international attention to the situation and also to request food assistance to feed the refugees. The U.S. administration of Richard Nixon supplied arms to Western Pakistan. The Indian Government supplied arms and training to the guerillas in East Pakistan. As a result, Western Pakistan attacked India on 3 December 1971. The war only lasted 15 days, but it severed Pakistan. East Pakistan was now a separate country, which would be known as Bangladesh.

State Of Emergency

Indira reached the height of her popularity in 1971 after India won the war with neighboring Pakistan. However, several years later, protesters began demonstrations because of India's poor standard of living and high inflation. In the mid-1970s, a political opponent who lost an election to Indira charged that she used illegal practices during the campaign. A court found her guilty in 1975 and ordered Indira to leave office.

The court convicted her of electoral corruption because she used government jeeps and officials during a campaign. The election was to be annulled, and she would be prohibited from holding any office for six years.

India was already amid turmoil due to several droughts in the early '70s. Serious food shortages resulted, prices rose and the country faced strikes and riots. She responded by placing the country in a state of emergency on 26 June 1975. Normal democratic practices were suspended.

- The press faced strict censorship.
- Political opponents were placed in prison.
- Strikes and sit ins were declared illegal.
- Constitutional rights were ignored.

In addition to suspending civil liberties, Indira announced a new program for agricultural reform and to bring prices down. In her opinion, the changes made were legal because the ruling Congress Party had expanded her powers under the Maintenance of Internal Security Act (MISA). Other countries viewed India as moving from democracy to dictatorship.

Less than five months after the initial conviction, the Indian Supreme Court dismissed the charges against Indira on 5 November 1975. Instead of lifting the state of emergency, however, she announced a month later that the next election would be in 1977.

One year and seven months after the state of emergency was declared, it was relaxed and general elections resumed.

In March 1977, Indira was defeated and a new prime minister elected. The following year in 1978, she was elected to parliament. And in January 1980, she re-captured her former position as prime minister in an election.

Throughout India's history, a major concern facing leaders is the strained relations among various religious groups. The majority of India's population is Hindu, followed by Islam and a small percentage comprises Sikhs, Christians, Buddhism, Jainism,

Judaism and Zoroastrianism. In the northern part of India is a region called Punjab. This is where Sikhism was created, which consists of the belief in one God, like Islam, and the belief in reincarnation, like Hinduism.

The Golden Temple

In the early 1980s, the Sikhs demanded an independent state for themselves from India and resorted to terrorism to gain attention. They established a base in a holy Sikh shrine, referred to as the Golden Temple.

Violence continued to increase in the surrounding area around Amritsar, where the temple is located, about 248 miles (397 kilometers) northwest of New Delhi.

The temple had become more of a fortress where terrorists lived, and pilgrims still tried to visit. The terrorists killed a member of congress and then vowed to kill one public official every day.

Indira sent 15,000 troops into Punjab. Of that amount, 5,400 hundred went to the Golden Temple located on a 72-acre complex. The militants had a stockpile of mortars, rockets and anti-tank missiles.

An estimated 600 to 1,300 Sikhs and soldiers were killed during the clash in June of 1984.

Returning To Her Roots

Four months later, Indira decided to visit her ancestor's homeland in Kashmir. She wanted to see an old chinar tree that she had loved as a child. The leaves of a chinar tree turn crimson in the fall. Within India, the chinar tree is commonly referred to as the universal mother of trees. When Indira went to see the leaves of her beloved tree changing colors, she found that the tree had died sometime earlier, and there were no leaves left to change color.

She returned home, and on the morning of 31 October 1984, Indira was excited about an interview she was scheduled to give to the British actor Peter Ustinov. Since she was going to appear on camera, she had not worn her bulletproof vest.

As she walked the path to the neighboring building where the interview would take place, one of her bodyguards pulled out a weapon and fired multiple times. A second body guard began shooting also. Combined, they had shot her 16 times.

Ironically, she was shot by two men whose job was to protect her. Her own bodyguards assassinated her because they were Sikh and wanted revenge on the attack at their shrine. The two assassins and one accomplice were charged, convicted and all sentenced to death.

The Aftermath

As news of Indira's assassination spread, Hindus began attacking innocent Sikhs in their homes and on the streets. Indira's son Rajiv implored for the violence to stop, stating that his mother would not have approved of the reaction.

Rajiv Gandhi became the next prime minister of India, following in the footsteps of the Nehru-Gandhi legacy. When campaigning for election in 1991, Rajiv was assassinated. His wife, named Sonia Gandhi, continued the legacy when she became president of the Congress Party.

In June 2006, Congress President Sonia Gandhi inaugurated an Indian Islamic Cultural Centre designed to promote religious understanding. The land had originally been set aside in 1981 and then a foundation stone was lain in 1984 by Indira. Plans for the centre had been set aside after her assassination. Nearly 22 years later, the centre became a reality during a time when understanding of Islam and other religions is as needed as ever before.

In July 2006, the Indian Government announced that compensation would be paid to Sikhs who were caught in the anti-Sikh violence – following the assassination of Indira. The recommendation for payment is based on a rehabilitation package as analyzed by a commission. A retired judge handled the commission to investigate violence against Sikhs in New Delhi and Uttar Pradesh.

Indira would have most likely approved of the payments and appreciated the religious cultural centre. . . .

After Indira's death, an editorial in The Indian Express stated:

> "Both our politics and our political debates have centered around her. We have been for her, or against her. Either way, we have been mesmerized by her."

INDIRA GANDHI (India)		
Born: 19 November 1917	Died: 31 October 1984	Age: 66

"Education is a liberating force, and in our age it is also a democratizing force, cutting across the barriers of caste and class, smoothing out inequalities imposed by birth and other circumstances."

~ Indira Gandhi

(From the Indira Gandhi National Open University site, http://www.ignou.ac.in)

YITZHAK RABIN

Before the territory was reclaimed as the state of Israel, a child was born in Jerusalem who would grow up with a love of the land and with a dedication to serve. That child, born on the 1 March 1922, was named Yitzhak after his mother's recently deceased father.

Yitzhak's father, named Nehemiah Robichov, changed his last name to Rabin in 1917. He had already left his native Russia for the United States and then went to Palestine. He was part of a group called the Jewish Legion fighting to free Palestine from Turkish control during World War I.

While defending people in Jerusalem, Nehemiah met Rosa Cohen who was helping with the wounded during a riot. They married in 1921 in Israel's port city of Haifa. Yitzhak's parents were known as Zionists. They belonged to an international movement who believed in re-establishing the state of Israel in the area known at that time – as Palestine. Zion refers to the site of Solomon's Temple in the city of Jerusalem. Some Zionists are religious, and some are politically influenced by the ideas of socialism.

His parents believed strongly in social responsibility. His father held trade union meetings at their apartment. His mother worked as an accountant while Golda Meir was a cashier at the same construction company. She also volunteered her time to help the Jewish workers of Tel Aviv, where they had moved about a year after Yitzhak's birth.

Both parents belonged to an organization called the Haganah, dedicated to defending the Jewish people. As a result of their military activities, sometimes the shower was so full of ammunition that it could not be used for getting cleaned up.

Yitzhak had one sibling, a sister named Rachel, who was three years younger than him. Sometimes their parents' military duties called them away for several weeks at a time. They would be dependant on neighbors to help look after them.

Yitzhak did not like this situation, but he understood it. When he finished kindergarten, his parents sent him to the School for Workers' Children. Years later, he would write in his autobiography of the trauma of going to school the first few days without his mother and fighting back tears.

> "My character (which I seem to have inherited from her) always showed a tendency toward withdrawal, but soon I was deeply involved in school – though then, as now, I did not show my feelings or share them with others."

He attended the workers' school for eight years, which involved not only education but also the students worked a vegetable garden, cooked their own meals and washed the dishes. The school also housed a carpentry shop for projects.

For his next level of schooling, Yitzhak attended several different agricultural schools over the years. These were popular at the time with the idea of transforming the desert into a fruitful land. It was also a way to encourage the youth to embrace and lay claim to the land.

In 1936, Palestine was the scene of riots and attacks by Arabian fighters. Yitzhak's high school was attacked several times, and the students helped defend it.

In November 1937, a relative came to retrieve Yitzhak from school. His mother was in a hospital in Tel Aviv. She was conscious but couldn't speak. While she had heart problems for years, she also had developed cancer, which did take her life now at the age of 47.

He graduated from school in August 1940 at the top of his class. World War II was going on at the time, and Yitzhak did not feel he could leave his country, even though he had received a college scholarship from the University of California at Berkley in the United States.

Instead, he joined a kibbutz, which refers to a collective farm used to help settle an area. One day, during supper at the kibbutz, a local commander recruited Yitzhak for the underground militia of the Haganah. Within the Haganah was an elite military unit called the Palmach dedicated to special operations.

Refugee Camps

After World War II ended in June 1945, illegal immigration became a top priority. Within the continent of Europe, an estimated 250,000 Jewish refugees had no place to go and were held in camps, where they became known as "displaced persons."

Thousands of Holocaust survivors sailed off the coast of Europe headed toward Palestine. Over a three-year period, more than 60 ships made the trip. The majority were intercepted by the British Navy. Marked as a "Haganah Ship – Jewish State" one boat displayed the following banner:

> "We survived Hitler. Death is no stranger to us. Nothing can keep us from our Jewish homeland."
>
> (From the book "Yitzhak Rabin – Israel's Soldier Statesman")

When the British intercepted the ships, they would be deported to Cyprus and in some cases – Germany. The British who controlled Palestine at this time only allowed 71,000 Jewish immigrants and then closed the borders, even to the Holocaust refugees.

At only 23 years of age, Yitzhak was selected to be one of the leaders to liberate refugees from a camp. The camp located in Athlit was on the Mediterranean shore about eight miles (13 kilometers) southwest of Haifa.

A Palmach group first infiltrated the camp by posing as teachers and welfare workers. Once inside, they organized the refugees for the mission and also overtook the Arab guards and broke the firing pins off of the rifles. Under the cover of a moonless night, about 200 Palmach troops entered to rescue the refugees. In his autobiography, Yitzhak wrote:

> "These people were survivors of the Holocaust, the few snatched from the conflagration. We would never be able to forgive ourselves if any harm were to befall them."

In planning for the mission, there were two factors they had not foreseen. One factor was the refugees who refused to leave behind the only possessions they had, which represented their worldly belongings. The other situation involved the babies and the children of the Holocaust who their parents struggled to carry.

The first group of a 100 refugees left with the other leader of the operation. It was decided that Yitzhak would wait for the last group of the refugees. A British truck came by and opened fire. The Palmach responded, resulting in the death of a British sergeant.

With the second and final group, the soldiers took over for the parents and placed the young children on their shoulders. Yitzhak scooped up a terrified Jewish child. As they traveled along, the frightened child urinated down Yitzhak's back. Yitzhak kept on moving. To reach the kibbutz, they had to climb 1,800 feet (540 meters) up Mount Carmel. There was no time for stopping.

It was daylight by the time they reached the kibbutz. Two scouts went ahead and found a hole in the British line. The refugees were quickly led through. The Palmach hid their weapons in previously designated caches since it was illegal for them to have guns and rifles.

To help the refugees blend in, the Haganah had organized and brought in buses transporting 15,000 Jewish civilians. They entered the kibbutz and protected the refugees in a sea of humanity. Once the British entered, they could not identify the refugees from the civilians. The refugees stayed, and the only casualty was the one British officer.

Leah Schlossberg

Leah Schlossberg was a 15-year-old student in the summer of 1943. She saw a young man who had the bearing of a Palmach soldier. She would later write in her autobiography:

> "To me, he looked just like King David himself."

This encounter happened in an ice cream parlor in Tel Aviv. The chance meetings grew until they started making plans to get together.

In 1945, she graduated from school and also joined the Palmach. She became stationed in the same kibbutz as Yitzhak. The Palmach members wore no uniforms nor insignia there, so the British could not identify them from the civilian members of the kibbutz.

One duty Leah performed in her early days was taking care of the tea samovar in the dining hall. Yitzhak would often look for her there on Friday evenings.

Leah's extroverted nature worked well with Yitzhak's introverted tendencies. He had confided in her regarding his first leadership operation with the refugee camp. She had seen his fear beforehand and rejoiced in the victory afterward.

A little more than five years after they had met, Leah and Yitzhak married in Tel Aviv on 23 August 1948. This was during a second truce in Israel's War of Independence. The honeymoon was postponed for six months but eventually was held in Naharia, Israel.

Statehood

Exhausted from World War II and the Jewish resistance, the British turned over the decision of the future of the territory to a United Nations Special Committee on Palestine. On the 29 November 1947, the United Nations (U.N.) announced the country would be divided into a Jewish state and an Arab state.

Jerusalem would not be part of either state but rather a separate "international zone." Several days after the U.N. announcement, the British advised that they would pull out of Palestine on 15 May 1948. The day after the U.N. announcement, groups of Arab militia (irregulars) started attacking Jewish settlements. There was no formal declaration of war, but that's when the fighting began.

The day the British pulled out was considered the first day of Israel's modern-day statehood on 15 May 1948. About the same time, five regular armies of the surrounding Arab countries began attacking Israel's borders.

With the creation of statehood, an official army was formed called the Israel Defense Forces (IDF). The Palmach units were absorbed into the new army so there would be one official army.

In early 1949, armistice talks began, and an agreement was signed. This war ended, and Israel received admittance as a member of the United Nations.

In the 1950s, the Rabins first child was born – a daughter, named Dalia, and the second child – born five years later – was a son, named Yuval. Yitzhak convinced Leah to be a full-time mom because he didn't want their children to feel "abandoned" due to his activities. While the family grew, so did Yitzhak's responsibilities with the Israel Defense Forces. This served him well for an important future test – of the longest six days.

The Six-Day War

As Israel celebrated its 19th Independence Day on 15 May 1967, Egypt deployed 500 tanks in the Sinai. Television broadcasts from Egypt could be picked up in Israel, where they viewed the Egyptian President Gamal Nasser screaming "Death to the Jews! We'll throw them into the sea!" Eight days later, Egypt closed the Strait of Tiran to Israeli ships.

On 30 May 1967, Jordan signed a military pact to support Egypt. The Arab goal had been announced to exterminate Israel.

Israeli troops started marching to their borders. They were outnumbered three to one. For the Israelis to have a chance, they felt they must first command the air and not wait for a strike.

Yitzhak would later write:

> "We knew that initiating an attack would provide us with great advantages – especially in terms of the air war because the side that achieved air superiority would immediately better its odds in all aspects of the land and sea battles as well."

Israel's strategy was to put Egypt's airfields, runways, planes, radar and maintenance operations out of commission. At 7:45 a.m. on 5 June 1967, the first wave of Israeli's fighter aircraft departed for Egypt. In three waves, more than 60 aircraft took off at a time in each group. Twelve fighters stayed behind to protect Israeli air space. Within three hours, the Egyptian air force was decimated.

By 11:50 a.m., that same day, Syria, Jordan and Iraqi air forces began hitting Israeli targets, including Yitzhak's own neighborhood. These air forces were also defeated, and on the first day of battle, Israel brought down 400 Arab planes. Yitzhak wrote:

> "The elimination of Arab air power was of decisive importance for morale."

On 7 June 1967, Israeli soldiers fought Jordanians for control of Jerusalem's Old City. By 10 a.m., the control of the Temple Mount was in Israeli hands. The Israeli paratroopers now controlled the Western Wall. This is the only wall that still remains of Solomon's Temple, the only wall left of Zion.

The significance of having this under Jewish control was so great that soldiers wept, overcome with joy. That day, Yitzhak had been asked to accompany Defense Minister Moshe Dayan. They met General Uzi Narkiss, commander of the operation, and marched together through the Lion's Gate, the entrance to the ancient treasures of Israel's historic past.

During this same day, four Israeli aircraft flew over a ship off the coast of Israel. No country identification could be seen on the vessel, so they thought it must be Egyptian. The fighters attacked, and an Israeli ship sent a torpedo.

The damaged vessel was the United States Ship (USS) Liberty. The Americans could not identify the planes that had attacked them, and thought perhaps it was the Soviets. U.S. President Lyndon Johnson was weighing if U.S. aircraft should strike the Soviet fleet in the Mediterranean.

Before it escalated to that level, the Israeli and U.S. governments discovered the real situation.

(Israel had previously requested that U.S. vessels stay off the Israeli coastline. This was communicated to the Sixth Fleet regarding the request. But word didn't make it to the USS Liberty.)

On board the USS Liberty, 32 persons had been killed, including American Jews chosen for their Hebrew and English language skills. Later on, because of the attack, the Israeli government gave $13 million dollars to the families of those killed or wounded.

As a result of the Six-Day War, Israel lost 777 soldiers and more than 2,500 were wounded. Civilian deaths and casualties ranged from 800 to 3,000.

By 10 June 1967, the cease-fire went into effect. Israel had significantly increased its land size and buffer zone around the country. Israel now controlled:

- The West Bank
- The Gaza Strip
- The Sinai Peninsula
- The Golan Heights
- Jerusalem

The next day, Sunday, 11 June 1967, was one of the worst days. As chief of staff, Yitzhak Rabin oversaw the communication to the families of those killed. Everyone in Israel waited to see if a taxi pulled in front of the home. Representatives of the Ministry of Defense would knock on the door with the news. The country held a 30-day period of mourning to honor those lost due to the war.

After a long military career, Yitzhak now looked to the future for the next challenge.

The Diplomat

Because Israel used a pre-emptive strike in the Six-Day War, U.S. President Johnson froze arm sales to Israel, even those previously agreed to.

In the interest of Israel's future security, Yitzhak viewed the relationship with the United States as of strategic importance in obtaining modern weapons and financial support.

Yitzhak approached the current Israeli Prime Minister Levi Eshkol to lobby for the job of diplomat to the United States. Even though Yitzhak was not known for his social graces, he said, "I'm confident that my military and political background as chief of staff will make up for any deficiencies in diplomatic experience."

Yitzhak was selected, and the month before his arrival, the Prime Minister Eshkol was in the United States lobbying for weapons. President Johnson made a commitment to sell 50 McDonnell Douglas F-4 Phantom jets. However, it would take a while for this to actually transpire. Yitzhak, Leah and their son, Yuval, arrived in Washington, D.C., in February 1968. Their daughter, Dalia, stayed behind because she was graduating from high school and was then required to enter the army.

The U.S. administration delayed the sale of the fighter aircraft and requested concessions before implementing the plan. The final approval came from President Johnson in January 1969 before his term expired.

Because of his military background, Yitzhak got to ride in a Phantom fighter jet. He visited a U.S. underground command post and saw the communications systems of nuclear submarines. He was asked his opinion on the advantages of different weapons.

During his five-year stay as a diplomat, he spoke at all of America's major military schools. He also spoke at many non-military campuses as well. His lectures would often be preceded by a bomb threat to the university. The threats did not deter Yitzhak from speaking. None of the bomb scares turned out to be real.

On 1 March 1973, Yitzhak and then Prime Minister Golda Meir met with U.S. President Richard Nixon and Secretary of State Henry Kissinger. The president confirmed the U.S. commitment to Israel. More than $500 million in weapons would be sent to Israel in the next few years. President Nixon remembered Yitzhak's birthday was that day and also that he would soon be leaving his post for return to Israel.

Yom Kippur

The Rabin family had already returned to Israel. About 8:30 a.m. on Saturday, 6 October 1973, Yitzhak received an unexpected call. The staff of Defense Minister Dayan had called to schedule a meeting at 3 p.m. that afternoon for all former chiefs of staff. Not only was this unusual for a Saturday, but even more so since it was also Yom Kippur.

Yom Kippur is one of the holiest days of the Jewish year. It is viewed as a day of fasting and of atonement or making amends. However, there would be no making amends on that day. Air-raid sirens blasted that afternoon. Egyptians crossed the Suez Canal and attacked Israel. Syrian soldiers gathered in the Golan Heights.

Yitzhak was on the sidelines during this battle. He was asked and agreed to take charge of a war loan drive for money that the government was desperate to have.

The Yom Kippur War lasted 23 days and came at a great cost. More than 2,700 Israelis died and from 7,500 – 9,000 soldiers were wounded. The cost ranged from $9 to $10 billion, and inflation soared in the small country.

Prime Minister

In June 1974, Yitzhak became Israel's first native-born prime minister and also the country's youngest at 52 years of age. Less than two weeks after assuming his new role, Yitzhak and his staff prepared for an unprecedented event in Israel's history – the visit of a U.S. president. When President Nixon arrived on 16 June 1974, Israeli citizens lined the road from the airport to the city of Jerusalem.

In addition to international issues, Yitzhak's office would be taking a look at domestic concerns as well. This included:

- Reducing the government budget
- Devaluing Israel's currency
- Banning imported cars and luxury goods for six months
- Overhauling the tax system

Even with the changes, the Israelis remained the highest taxed people of any country. And terrorism still grew by the Palestine Liberation Organization (PLO) against Israel.

Yitzhak's government worked to reinforce the military, strengthen the economy and solve social problems. One of the trickiest problems he would encounter was yet to come.

Operation Entebbe

On 27 June 1976, terrorists hijacked an Air France plane and redirected it to land in Uganda. The terrorists freed the French crew and all non-Jewish passengers. This left 83 Israeli hostages.

The Palestinian hijackers demanded the release of 53 convicted terrorists; the majority were in Israeli prisons, but six were in Germany, five in Kenya and one each in France and Switzerland. If the terrorists in prison were not released, executions would begin in 48 hours. Through negotiations, the deadline became extended, and an unusual rescue mission authorized by Yitzhak began.

A rehearsal of the rescue operations was held at Sharm el-Sheikh. The real mission began the next morning, on the 3 July 1976, a lead Hercules C-130 cargo plane left for Entebbe, Uganda. Inside were a rescue team, two military vehicles and a black Mercedes – identical to the personal car of Uganda dictator Idi Amin. Two additional cargo planes carried reinforcements, and a fourth one was meant to bring the hostages back. The Hercules cargo planes were escorted as far as possible by fighter F-4 Phantoms. The other aircraft needed were two Boeing 707s – one was designated as a command post and the other as an airborne hospital, landed and refueled in nearby Nairobi, Kenya.

After more than a seven-hour flight, the Hercules cargo planes landed at 23:01 hours at the Entebbe Airport. The rear cargo ramp dropped from the first plane and out drove the black Mercedes flying Ugandan flags. It was escorted by two vehicles with Israeli soldiers dressed in Ugandan uniforms. When approached by real Ugandan sentries, the commandos opened fire with silenced Berettas.

The first Hercules plane filled with hostages took off in just under an hour after landing. The last plane followed 40 minutes later amid bullets and explosions.

The successful operation resulted in these casualties: one Israeli commando, three hostages at the airport and one later who was already in a hospital in Uganda and all six hijackers. No terrorists who were held in prison were released that day.

At 2 a.m., Yitzhak was already waiting at the Israeli airport. He greeted the freed hostages and the soldiers upon their arrival.

The Bank Accounts

In March 1977, an Israeli newspaper published a story that the Rabins had joint bank accounts (checking and savings) in the United States. The reason why this was considered news is because of a law forbidding Israeli citizens from having foreign currency abroad, unless they were living overseas.

The bank accounts had been opened while living in the United States but not closed upon departure. When they returned to Israel, the combined accounts had $21,121 in them. No additional deposits had been made, and several withdrawals had taken place until the remaining balance was down to $2,000.

Most citizens viewed it as more of a technicality than a major offense. Yitzhak whose name was also on the account was assessed a minor fine. Leah who wrote the family checks was told to appear in court. On 17 April 1977, the evidence was presented. Leah would later write in her memoirs:

> "The judge gave me a lecture that many found outrageously stern and the choice of paying a 250,000 Israeli-pound fine – approximately the price of a decent condominium in those days –

or serving a year in jail. We paid the fine with the help of money borrowed from friends, whom we later repaid."

The fine was the equivalent of about $27,000 U.S. dollars. Hundreds of citizens sent letters and some even included checks, which they returned.

The Rabins decided not to appeal, and the case was closed. Even though he was not asked to, Yitzhak felt he should resign as prime minister under the circumstances. Two days after his resignation, he attended a soccer match in Tel Aviv. He received a standing ovation from the crowd at Bloomfield Stadium.

The Peace Process

During part of the 1980s, Yitzhak served as defense minister. Then in 1992, he became prime minister again while still serving as head of defense. Over the course of years and numerous conflicts, Yitzhak changed into more of a seeker of peace than a soldier. He knew that any lasting peace will in reality take decades to accomplish.

However, in the early 1990s, his government and the Palestine Liberation Organization (PLO) entered into negotiations. Yitzhak and his team made these important contributions to the peace process.

In 1993, the Israeli government entered into unconventional peace talks in Oslo, Norway. Two private individuals began negotiations with the PLO and were later joined by two government experts. An Oslo agreement was formed, requiring Israel to recall military personnel from the Gaza Strip and the West Bank city of Jericho by April of 1994.

On 9 September 1993, Yassir Arafat wrote a letter to Yitzhak stating that the PLO recognized Israel's right to exist. This was the first time such a document was received from the PLO.

On 10 September 1993, Yitzhak responded by recognizing the PLO. Then both leaders and their foreign ministers joined U.S. President Bill Clinton on the White House lawn to sign the document.

On 26 October 1994, Yitzhak signed a peace treaty with the Kingdom of Jordan, ending a state of war, technically since 1948.

Also in October 1994, it was announced that Yitzhak along with Shimon Peres, Israel's foreign minister and PLO Chairman Yassir Arafat would share in the Nobel Peace Prize. On the 10 December

1994, they all went to Oslo for the ceremony. During his remarks, Yitzhak said:

> "The profession of soldiering embraces a certain paradox. We take the best and bravest of our young men into the army. We supply them with equipment that costs a fortune. We rigorously train them for the day when they must do their duty – and we expect them to do it well. Yet we fervently pray that day will never come – that the planes will never take flight, the tanks will never move forward, the soldiers will never mount the attacks for which they have been trained so well."
>
> (Reported in the book "Rabin – Our Life, His Legacy")

Yitzhak and Shimon decided to pool their prize money and establish a fund to promote peace. In 1995, the peace talks continued under the name of Oslo II. In this framework, the West Bank would be divided into three zones with varying degrees of Palestinian or Israeli control.

On 28 September 1995, Yitzhak and Arafat were back at the U.S. White House with President

Bill Clinton. Also attending were King Hussein of Jordan and Egyptian President Hosni Mubarak, plus the foreign ministers of all the countries participating in the agreement.

With the Oslo II agreement signed, it was now debated on 5 October 1995 in the Israeli Parliament. The agreement met with strong opposition and included a 15-hour debate in the Knesset. The agreement barely passed with a vote of 61 to 59.

Despite Yitzhak's plans, a minority group of Israelis did not support his efforts toward peace. His decision to stop building new Jewish settlements in the West Bank and to return territory remained unpopular with the opposition.

Right-wing Israeli parties held a protest shouting "Rabin is a traitor." They had created fake posters of Yitzhak wearing an SS (Nazi) uniform. And then they burned the posters. An estimated 20,000 to 30,000 protesters voiced their opposition in Zion Square.

Song For Peace

A former mayor of Tel Aviv wanted to show that more Israelis supported the peace process by organizing a rally. It would be held on a Saturday evening on the 4

November 1995 outside in front of Tel Aviv's City Hall.

Yitzhak wasn't sure it was a good idea. He was afraid that not many people would come. The organizer assured him not to worry. He had arranged 500 buses to bring supporters from all over the country. This would show the nationwide support needed for the movement.

Yitzhak wore a dark suit. He and Leah rode in the backseat of a special armored silver Cadillac, which was used for high-risk security occasions.

At the peace rally, Yitzhak surrounded by security men asked the city police chief how large the crowd was.

It was more than 100,000. Some thought possibly as many as 200,000 people. The crowd stretched as far as they could see. Yitzhak filled with joy at the size of the group – the proof that the majority of citizens did want peace. This crowd shouted "Rabin, we love you!" They had posters and banners with positive messages.

This was a victory rally for Oslo II with foreign dignitaries attending from Egypt, Jordan and Morocco. Shimon Peres spoke, and then Yitzhak hugged him in an unusual show of affection, taking everyone by surprise. Then he started his own remarks.

> "I was a military man for 27 years. I fought as long as there was no chance for peace. Today I believe that there is a chance for peace, a good chance."
>
> (Reported in the book "The Rabin Memoirs")

After the speeches, a popular singer Miri Aloni joined the politicians and organizers on stage. Those on stage received song sheets with the lyrics to "The Song Of Peace" ("Shir La'Shalom").

After this song concluded, Yitzhak carefully folded the lyric sheet and placed it inside his jacket pocket. A second singer came out and performed "To Cry For You," dedicated to those who didn't live to see peace as a reality. Then the rally concluded with Israel's national anthem called "Hatikvah" (meaning "The Hope").

After the rally was over, Yitzhak gave the organizer a big hug. He thanked him for one of the best days of his life. In a state of euphoria, Yitzhak and Leah headed back toward the car. Leah was still on the stairs when Yitzhak was starting to get into the car.

"Where's Leah?" he asked. Then, three shots fired off while someone yelled: "It's not real."

But they were real. Yitzhak had been hit by two bullets and his bodyguard by one. They got into the Cadillac, and the driver sped to the hospital.

Meanwhile, police officers captured the gunman. Leah, who was not injured, was taken in a separate security car to Shabak (General Security Service) headquarters as normal protocol. They didn't seem to have the details yet of what was transpiring. She called her daughter to advise her of the little she knew. Leah told the security staff to take her to the hospital. Leah would write later:

> "All the efforts at the hospital had been valiant but futile. Yitzhak was actually dead two minutes after the shooting when he collapsed in the car, the bloodstained copy of the Song of Peace folded in his pocket."
>
> (Reported in the book "Rabin – Our Life, His Legacy")

The assassin was an Israeli student and a religious extremist. He would be convicted and sentenced to life in prison.

Yitzhak's coffin lay in state at the Knesset with the Israeli flag, which bears the Star of David. In the first 24 hours, a quarter of a million people filed past the coffin. He was buried the following day on 6 November 1995 in the national cemetery of Mount Herzl next to the previous prime ministers of Israel and those who founded the country and Zionism.

Shimon Peres would implement the Oslo II accord, carrying on the legacy. On 10 December 1995, a memorial rally was held at Madison Square Garden in New York City. Shimon and Leah spoke at the rally where about 15,000 persons attended. To the crowd, Leah expressed the words in remembrance of her husband:

"Yitzhak Rabin loved you."

YITZHAK RABIN (Israel)		
Born: 1 March 1922	Died: 4 November 1995	Age: 73

"What begins as a threat to the Jews is soon a menace to the entire world. It is but a short step between a knifing in Jerusalem and bombing the World Trade Center in New York. All of this has influenced the pattern of our position in the coming years. One hand we will outstretch in peace, the other we will keep poised on the trigger."

~ Yitzhak Rabin

(Reported in "The Rabin Memoirs")

AHMAD SHAH MASSOOD (THE LION OF PANJSHIR)

Afghanistan, a country slightly smaller than the state of Texas, has become known as the nation with the most refugees living outside its own borders. For more than 20 years, wars and human rights abuses have led to Afghans leaving their homeland when possible. At different points in time, anywhere from two million to six million refugees have sought shelter, primarily in Iran and Pakistan.

One of the individuals who would not leave his homeland behind was called the Lion of Panjshir. His real name has been spelled multiple ways, depending on the country or organization reporting his activities. He has been referred to as Ahmad Shah Massood, Ahmed Shah Massoud or Masoud or a combination of these. He was born in the 1950s during the rule of King Zahir Shah while Afghanistan was experiencing a longer period of stability. Ahmad was born in a village called Bazarak, located less than a mile from Martyr's Hill up the Panjshir River. His father, Dost Mohammad Khan, served as a colonel in the Afghan Army. The family lived in Bazarak his first five years of life before moving to Herat, where his father became the chief of police. The next family move was to the country's capital of Kabul.

He was considered a gifted student. He attended religious and academic schools. He spoke his native language of Dari (a dialect of Persian) but also became fluent in French, Urdu and Pashto. His family was part of an ethnic group known as the Tajiks. Their religion like the majority of the population in Afghanistan is Islamic. It is customary for men to have more than one wife, if desired. His father had three. From one of the marriages, Ahmad had three full-blooded brothers.

After graduating from high school, Ahmad studied engineering at Kabul University, where he would become a member of an Islamic student group. He joined a political movement headed by a man who would become his mentor, Burhanuddin Rabbani.

In 1973, the king was overthrown by his brother-in-law in a bloodless coup. Five years later, the brother-in-law and his family were murdered when the communists took control of the government.

During this period, Ahmad and many other young Muslims went to Pakistan for military training. He came back in 1975 to participate in raids against Afghan Army posts. Then, he left and returned to Afghanistan again in 1978 after the communist takeover.

The Letter

With his return home, Ahmad wrote a letter to the different villages in the Panjshir Valley. In one village named Dasht-i-Debat, the tribal elders called a meeting of the men in the village. They read the letter aloud, which stated that the Communist regime wanted to change the Afghan culture. It was time for the Afghan people to defend themselves.

As a result of the letter, about 100 men organized themselves in the village, even those without weapons or military experience. Another nearby village named Safichir also started organizing. A month after the letter was received, Ahmad came with about 20 men. Ahmad was only about 26 and looked like one of the youngest in the group. In the book "The Lion's Grave," one of his commanders described Ahmad as an honest man. "He didn't seem to be interested in money, and he acted like a leader."

Dasht-i-Debat, Safichir and Paian became the first three villages to organize, but they would not be the last. Ahmad was a leader who could organize guerilla insurgencies. Outside metropolitan areas, much of Afghanistan was ruled by tribal systems. Villagers felt most loyal to their respective tribal chiefs. Under Islamic law, believers should bear arms when requested by their leaders.

In 1979, the Soviets invaded Afghanistan to help support the Communist regime. The United States government started providing covert funds to help train forces through the Pakistani secret service. This agency was known as the Inter Services Intelligence (ISI) and was comprised of Muslims opposed to the atheism of a Communist regime.

During the 10-year Soviet occupation, it was estimated there was a huge exodus of 5 million Afghans who left the country. While the occupation continued, 1983 to 1984 were suppose to be truce years for Ahmad and the Soviets. However, they tried to assassinate him on two different occasions during that time. Both attempts failed.

The Lion Of Panjshir

Ahmad's reputation developed as a soldier and as a brilliant military commander during the Soviet occupation. His ability and prowess to hold onto his homeland of the Panjshir Valley earned him the name – the Lion of Panjshir. Ahmad's charismatic appeal enabled him to reach a wide variety of groups across ethnic tribes.

Ahmad would strive to pay his field commanders by controlling the flow of emeralds and gems from the mines located in the region. Profits from the gems would pay soldier salaries and purchase weapons.

After 10 years of fighting, Soviet troops withdrew in 1989. At the height of the occupation, an estimated 120,000 Soviet soldiers were in Afghanistan. To remember those killed or wounded in the Soviet / Afghani War, a holiday was created in Afghanistan on the 4 May. It is called Remembrance Day for the Martyrs and Disabled.

In 1992, Ahmad became defense minister in a new government where his political mentor,

Burhanuddin Rabbani, served as president. Fighting among the ethnic tribes and religious groups created vast damage to the city of Kabul. The groups fighting became known as the holy warriors or the mujahedeen. Human rights abuses were committed by all groups involved in the fighting. The tribes fought each other for several years while tens of thousands of civilians fled the city.

The Taliban

In 1994, a group of young warriors, known as the Taliban, started vying for power in Afghanistan. They referred to themselves as "God's Students." One theory is that the Taliban formed when a religious teacher named Mawlawi Mohammed Omar organized his students into a vigilante group to pursue some men believed to have assaulted three women. Another theory is that the Taliban started as a result of agents of Pakistan's secret service.

Also in 1994, the African country of Sudan came under pressure from Saudi Arabia and the United States to expel a terrorist known as Osama bin Laden. He left Sudan and became a guest of the Taliban. While in Afghanistan, his group known as al-Qaida set up terrorist training camps. Al-Qaida means "the law" or "the foundation." The Sunni Islamist organization works to eliminate "infidels" and foreign influences in Muslim countries. As the Taliban established itself, it proceeded to capture southern provinces of Afghanistan just by bribing commanders, without even fighting.

As the Taliban grew in strength, it was even able to overtake the ruling Afghan Government on 27 September 1996 in Kabul. The Taliban entered the city of Kabul on foot and also in tanks. They took control of the Presidential Palace and the Ministries of Defence, Security and Foreign Affairs. They took the former president who had been ousted in 1992 and his brother and killed them. Then, their bodies were left to hang from a concrete traffic post.

At this time, the Taliban declared itself as the legal government of Afghanistan; however, it was recognized by only a few countries, which would later drop their recognition of the Taliban.

The Taliban rule by an extreme interpretation of Shariah, also known as Islamic law, which is based on the Quran, the Islamic holy book. Kandahar is a city in Afghanistan with special religious significance. According to an article in the Christian Science Monitor, there is an ornate building in the center of the city with a vault made of streaked green and orange marble. Inside the vault is the cloak believed to have belonged to Muhammad, the Muslim prophet. In 1994, the Taliban leader Omar wore the cloak at a public rally. Afghan legend says that only a true leader can unlock the doors leading to where the cloak is kept. This was one of the few times that Omar went to a public event. He has one eye, after losing the other fighting Soviet forces. Since he does not go out in public that often, he has rarely been photographed.

The Taliban's Interpretation

Islam is the name of the only legal religion allowed in Afghanistan. Those who practice the Islamic religion are referred to as Muslims. The majority of the population is Sunni Muslim (roughly 85 to 90 percent) and the remaining 10 to 15 percent is Shiite Muslim.

The Taliban committed numerous human rights violations and placed the following rules on Muslims living in Afghanistan:

- Muslims must participate in five daily prayers. Prayers at mosques at noon on Friday are required for men. Females must pray at home because they aren't allowed in mosques.

- It is illegal to listen to music, to watch television or films or to have a computer.

- Schools are not allowed to teach girls over the age of eight. Those who are under eight will only be taught from the Quran.

- Playing chess and flying kites are not allowed.

- Photographs of humans are not allowed, and neither is playing with dolls or toy animals.

- Women can no longer attend universities and cannot work outside the home.

- A man's beard must be longer than holding a fist at the base of the chin. Long hair is not allowed for men, and they should also wear head coverings.

- Women need to wear a garment from head to toe known as a burqa. If a woman cannot afford to buy one, then she can never leave her home without the risk of being beaten by the religious police.

- Women must be escorted by a male relative whenever leaving home, which causes problems for those who have been widowed and lost relatives due to the fighting.

- Any home where a woman lives must have the windows painted over, so the occupants are not visible from the street.

- A hospital cannot treat both men and women; so most have been instructed to treat only men.

- Those who have committed adultery might be stoned to death or sentenced to 100 lashes.

- Amputations and executions are held in public.

Ban On Poppies

In July 2000, the Taliban banned Afghan farmers from growing any more poppies. The poppies are a key ingredient in the creation of opium, and in some years, Afghanistan was the world's largest producer of the illegal drug. Farmers complied with the request and planted wheat, corn and onions instead.

The Taliban said it was offering to halt the production of opium poppies and in return wanted to receive international recognition as the real government of Afghanistan. A United Nations panel was not impressed. The United Nations wanted the Taliban to hand over the terrorist Osama bin Laden.

According to an article in The (London) Times, the United Nations believed the Taliban stopped the growing of poppies to drive up the prices of opium and heroin. Then, the Taliban sold its existing stockpiles at higher prices to buy weapons and to train terrorists.

In September 2000, the Taliban captured the city of Taloqan. This was a community of approximately 200,000 people in northern Afghanistan and also was serving as the headquarters for Ahmad. He re-assembled his headquarters in the village of Khoja Bahauddin, located near the border of Tajikistan.

The Taliban had taken control of 90 to 95 percent of Afghanistan by the early part of 2001. However, they had never been able to capture the Panjshir Valley controlled by the Lion. Ahmad worked with other ethnic groups to form an anti-Taliban stronghold, known as the United Front or Northern Alliance.

Buddhist Statues

Allies of Osama bin Laden were believed to have taken more control of the Taliban and ordered the destruction of Buddhist statues in March 2001 because they viewed the statues as idolatry. The Metropolitan Museum of Art in New York offered to buy the ancient relics. Instead, the Taliban proceeded to destroy the artifacts. All statues were destroyed within the Kabul Museum. There had been two towering statues of Buddha, dating back to the 3rd and 5th centuries, carved into the mountains in the province of Bamiyan, which the Taliban targeted and damaged by setting off explosives.

The International Community

Ahmad realized that he and other Afghans needed additional help. He traveled to Europe for the first time to ask for Western assistance in Afghanistan's war against terror. In April 2001, he addressed the European Parliament in Strasbourg, France. He also spoke with European officials and with members of the international media, warning that al-Qaida posed a threat to everyone, not just Afghanistan. He began to receive recognition as a statesman. While Osama bin Laden always positioned himself as representing Muslims, here was Ahmad representing moderate Islam.

His brother Ahmad Wali Massood worked as a diplomat in the Afghani embassy in London. In July

2001, his brother held a conference for Afghans in exile. Those attending passed a resolution endorsing the Lion for his work in Afghanistan and also for supporting democracy, women's issues and human rights.

Training Camps

Recruits went to al-Qadea training camps to learn skills that would be needed for terrorist-related activities. Attendees developed skills in the use of firearms, explosives, other weapons and knowledge of topography. As part of military life, they learned discipline. To test psychological fitness and commitment to jihad, they were subjected to numerous stresses.

One of the key facilities was the al Faruq camp near Kandahar. In mid-2000, seven operatives were chosen from the camp for a unique mission that would involve flying airplanes. They would join operatives who had been training at other facilities.

All of the recruits were sent to Saudi Arabia to apply for U.S. visas and then returned to Afghanistan for more training. This training occurred at the al Matar complex. It was at this facility, that they were instructed on how to storm a cockpit door, how to disarm air marshals and how to conduct a hijacking. They learned some English and started bodybuilding. To practice using knives, the trainees had to butcher a sheep and a camel.

When this training was completed, they went to Karachi, Pakistan, and then to Dubai in the United Arab Emirates. In late April 2001, the operatives started arriving in groups of two on tourist visas for the United States.

In the summer of 2001, Ahmad started receiving reports of Taliban and al-Qaida forces gathering along his northern front. Some reports estimated as many as 16,000 troops were gathering.

In early September, Ahmad and his staff flew over the area in a helicopter, so he could determine where best to station his men. On 9 September 2001, Ahmad and several of his men stayed up until 3 a.m., reading Persian poetry aloud. Classic Persian poetry remains an integral part of Afghan culture. Poetry competition events are even held.

Not long after Ahmad went to sleep that morning, he was awakened with the news that the Taliban had attacked his forces. Ahmad and one of his commanders discussed the situation on the phone until daybreak. Ahmad returned to sleep and was awakened at 9 a.m. for breakfast.

The Taliban had started retreating. Before leaving on a reconnaissance trip, Ahmad decided to meet with two Arab journalists who had been waiting to see him. They came with a letter of introduction from a group called the Islamic Observation Centre in London. It was agreed that Ahmad would see the journalists around noon that day. During the same time, he would also allow a small film company named Ariana to record the interview. This company had previously filmed interviews that Ahmad gave.

They met in the chief of security office of Ahmad's headquarters. The Ariana crew and the Arab team each set up their equipment. Ahmad used an orthopedic cushion to help relieve his chronic back pain.

Before starting the interview, Ahmad wanted to hear all of the questions and then he would answer. Questions were read in English and then translated into Persian by an ambassador. The majority of the questions referenced Osama bin Laden, which was unusual. "What will you do with Osama bin Laden if you take power?"

The ambassador questioned which news outlet they worked for? They responded that they were not journalists but representing Islamic centers throughout the world, meaning that they represented al-Qaida.

Ahmad responded with "Let's just get through with it." Suddenly, the room exploded. The ambassador, who lived through the attack, said later he saw a blue fire coming toward him and then he felt burning. He left the room for help and came back and saw that Ahmad was critically injured. An intelligence officer estimated that Ahmad died in about 30 seconds.

It was believed that the battery belt and / or the camera used were packed with explosives. The suicide bomber also died from the explosion.

Ahmad's body, the ambassador and others injured were transported by car to the helicopter pad. They all went to a hospital in Tajikistan. They agreed to keep Ahmad's assassination a secret by saying he was injured and recovering. The Arab who conducted the interview survived and was being held at Ahmad's headquarters. He escaped from the building and was then killed in pursuit.

The news of the attack spread to the United States. On 10 September 2001, the CIA was instructed there would be a "broad covert action program." This would include the use of lethal force against al-Qaida.

In Afghanistan on 10 September 2001, the Taliban offensive resumed against the Northern Alliance.

On 11 September 2001, the hijackers knew their mission. They had been instructed if they could not reach their U.S. targets, they would still crash the planes.

Four planes were hijacked that morning. Two hit the World Trade Center, which resulted in a fire and demolished both skyscrapers. Another plane hit the Pentagon. And the plane intended for the U.S. Capitol ended up in a rural Pennsylvania field after the passengers stormed the cockpit and confronted the hijackers.

Afterward

On 17 September 2001, the body of the Lion of Panjshir returned home to his final resting place – in the Panjshir Valley. Ahmad's tomb is in the hillside. A sign reads "Chief of the Martyr's Hill." He had returned to the place of his birth.

Ahmad's Afghan forces, the United States, and the international community joined together to remove many of the Taliban from Afghanistan before the end of 2001.

Following the fall of the Taliban, Kabul University reopened to both female and male students. More than two million Afghan refugees returned home.

An interim Afghan government was created, which bestowed upon Ahmad the title "Hero of the Afghan Nation." His youngest brother, Ahmad Wali Massood – the diplomat, returned to Kabul in the spring of 2002. He started a political party called the National Movement of Afghanistan.

Another brother named Ahmad Zia Massood, who had served as ambassador to Russia, was chosen as the vice presidential running mate for elections in 2004. He was elected vice president and Hamid Karzai as president of the Islamic Republic of Afghanistan. In 2005, 28 percent of the delegates elected to parliament were women.

Ahmad's family continues his legacy and will build on it for the future of the Afghan culture.

While the Lion has been lain to rest, his vision still remains of a free Afghanistan.

AHMAD SHAH MASSOOD (Afghanistan)		
Born: 9 January 1953	Died: 9 September 2001	Age: 48

"Any help that countries can give us for reconquering our country, we need it."

~ Ahmad Shah Massood
(Quoted in the BBC News)

LOOKING AT LEADERS

Being a leader means being focused. This enables you to accomplish your most important priorities. You cannot be all things to all people. Often, you will need to make choices – to reduce your involvement in some activities that do not contribute to your main goal. Sometimes you have to be selfish with your time to help others.

Observations while doing the research and writing on these leaders point out how tough it is on the family. For those who married and had children having a leader in the family meant less time for personal commitments.

One of the leaders extremely sensitive to this was Yitzhak Rabin, former prime minister of Israel. He grew up with both parents who worked and were activists involved in volunteer organizations. He understood their causes but still felt abandoned as a child. He tried to minimize this for his own family by asking his spouse to not work outside the home. She would be the full-time parent that he never had.

Some leaders are born into influential or powerful families and are groomed for their place in society like King Faisal of Saudi Arabia or Raoul Wallenberg, the Swedish diplomat. However, they must still find their own way, proving their wisdom and living up to family expectations.

Other leaders charted their own way without the benefit of a family with connections or money. This includes Anwar el-Sadat, former president of Egypt; Rosa Luxemburg, political activist / economist from Poland and Robert Capa, the photographer from Hungary.

For those serving in an activism role, it's not unusual to have spent time in prison while fighting against unfair laws. Some served more time than others. Some spent their last days in jail before execution. Here are some of the leaders who spent time in prison:

- Joan of Arc
- Stephen Bantu Biko
- Edith Cavell
- Michael Collins

- Indira Gandhi
- Martin Luther King Jr.
- Rosa Luxemburg
- José Rizal
- Anwar el-Sadat
- Sophie Scholl
- William Wallace
- Raoul Wallenberg

Being a leader is not about having a certain title, having money or having persons reporting to you. It's about having such strong convictions or a vision of something that you are relentless in your pursuit. Everyone profiled in this book ended up dying for what they believed in.

Please do not confuse these deaths with suicide missions because they are not. The author does not advocate suicide as a way to accomplish goals or demonstrate beliefs.

Many of the leaders obtained higher education or military service as a way to get started in life. The knowledge taught and the connections made proved valuable as they developed into leaders.

We all have the potential to be a leader if we so choose. The point of this book is to show you examples of previous leaders. And to show that you do not have to be perfect to accomplish great things as you can see by the profiles included here.

Those chosen for inclusion here represent different cultures, different religions, different political parties and different age groups.

You're never too young and you're never too old to be a leader. Now is the time to live a life of meaning and to make a contribution of what you value.

We each find our own path. We each have a unique journey to make. We each leave this life for an unknown destination. Let us leave something of meaning behind. ...

BIBLIOGRAPHY

Arc, Joan of

Gordon, Mary. "Joan of Arc." Penguin, 2000.

Hobbins, Daniel. "The Trial of Joan of Arc." Harvard University Press, 2005.

Trask, Willard R. (translator). "Joan of Arc – In Her Own Words." New York: Turtle Point Press, 1996.

Catholic Online (www.catholic.org), historical and biblical database about the Catholic Church.

Aziz, Faisal ibn Abdul

Beling, Willard A. (editor). "King Faisal and the Modernization of Saudi Arabia." London: Croom Helm, 1980.

Facey, William (editor). "The Kingdom Of Saudi Arabia." London and New Jersey: Stacey International, 1990. (Eighth edition).

Morrison, Terri; Conaway, Wayne A.; and Borden, George A. "Kiss, Bow, or Shake Hands." Holbrook, Massachusetts: Bob Adams, Inc., 1994.

Reed, Jennifer Bond. "The Saudi Royal Family." Philadelphia: Chelsea House Publishers, 2003.

Stefoff, Rebecca. "Faisal." New York and Philadelphia: Chelsea House Publishers, 1989.

Arab Net (www.arab.net), part of the Saudi Research and Marketing Group, a publisher of newspapers and magazines in the Kingdom of Saudi Arabia.

LexicOrient (www.i-cias.com), a Norway-based media company reporting on information in North Africa and the Middle East.

Presswire (www.presswire.com) "U.S. Scientists Honored For Lifetime Contributions In Hepatitis Research," 17 February 1998.

Biko, Steve Bantu

Biko, Steve. "I Write What I Like." San Francisco: Harper & Row, 1978.

Miller and Keane. Encyclopedia and Dictionary of Medicine. (3rd edition) W.B. Saunders, 1983.

Woods, Donald. "Biko." New York: Henry Holt And Company, 1987.

Capa, Robert

Capa, Robert. "Images Of War." New York: Grossman Publishers, 1964.

Kershaw, Alex. "Blood And Champagne." New York: St. Martin's Press, 2003.

Whelan, Richard. "Robert Capa." New York: Alfred A. Knopf, 1985.

National Public Radio (www.npr.org), "Morning Edition," 3 October 1997.

The Museum of Photographic Arts in San Diego (www.mopa.org).

Cavell, Edith

Bowie, Walter Russell. "Women Of Light." New York: Harper & Row, 1963.

De Leeuw, Adele. "Edith Cavell – Nurse, Spy Heroine." New York: G.P. Putnam's Sons, 1968.

McCain, John with Salter, Mark. "Character Is Destiny." New York: Random House, 2005.

Ryder, Rowland. "Edith Cavell." New York: Stein And Day, 1975.

Norwich Cathedral site (www.cathedral.org.uk).

Collins, Michael

Connolly, Colm. "The Illustrated Life Of Michael Collins." Boulder, Colorado: Roberts Rinehart Publishers, 1996.

Hart, Peter. "Mick – The Real Michael Collins." Viking, 2005.

Mackay, James. "Michael Collins – A Life." Edinburgh and London: Mainstream Publishing, 1996.

Ó Broin, León (editor). "In Great Haste." New York: St. Martin's Press, 1996.

O'Conner, Frank. "The Big Fellow." Dublin: Poolbeg Press, 1979.

Dollfuss, Engelbert

Berkley, George E. "Vienna and Its Jews." Lanham, Maryland: Madison Books, 1988.

Maass, Walter B. "Assassination In Vienna." New York: Charles Scribner's Sons, 1972.

Gandhi, Indira

Currimbhoy, Nayana. "Indira Gandhi." New York: Franklin Watts, 1985.

Dommermuth-Costa, Carol. "Indira Gandhi: Daughter Of India." Minneapolis: Lerner Publications Company, 2002.

Ganeri, Anita. "Indira Gandhi." Chicago: Heinemann Library, 2003.

Masani, Zareer. "Indira Gandhi: A Biography." New York: Thomas Y. Crowell, 1976.

Willcoxen, Harriett. "First Lady Of India: The Story Of Indira Gandhi." Garden City, N.Y.: Doubleday Signal Book, 1969.

Indira Gandhi National Open University site (www.ignou.ac.in).

King Jr., Martin Luther

Abernathy, Donzaleigh. "Partners To History: Martin Luther King Jr., Ralph David Abernathy, and the Civil Rights Movement. " New York: Crown Publishers, 2003.

Albert, Peter J. and Hoffman, Ronald (editors). "We Shall Overcome: Martin Luther King, Jr., And The Black Freedom Struggle." New York: Pantheon Books, 1990.

Burns, Stewart. "To The Mountaintop." Harper San Francisco, 2004.

Ching, Jacqueline. "The Assassination Of Martin Luther King Jr." New York: Rosen Publishing Group, 2002.

Fisher Phibbs, Cheryl (editor). "Pioneers of Human Rights." San Diego: Greenhaven Press, 2005.

Hansen, Drew W. "The Dream: Martin Luther King Jr., and the Speech that Inspired a Nation." New York: Ecco, 2003.

Hatt, Christine. "Martin Luther King Jr." Milwaukee: World Almanac Library, 2004.

King, Coretta Scott (selected by). "The Words Of Martin Luther King, Jr." New York: Newmarket Press, 1987.

King Jr., Martin Luther. "The Papers of Martin Luther King Jr." Berkeley: University of California Press, 2005

Kotz, Nick. "Judgment Days: Lyndon Baines Johnson, Martin Luther King Jr., And The Laws That Changed America." Houghton Mifflin Company, 2005.

British Broadcasting Corporation – BBC (www.bbc.co.uk).

Stanford University site, (www.stanford.edu).

Luxemburg, Rosa

Abraham, Richard. "Rosa Luxemburg – A Life For The International." Oxford / New York / Munich: Berg Publishers Limited, 1989.

Ettinger, Elzbieta. "Rosa Luxemburg – A Life." Boston: Beacon Press, 1986.

Nettl, J.P. "Rosa Luxemburg. " New York: Schocker Books, 1969.

The Australian (15 September 2006 edition): "Berlin monument to Marxist heroine." (www.theaustralian.news.com.au).

Massood, Ahmad Shah

Anderson, Jon Lee. "The Lion's Grave – Dispatches from Afghanistan." New York: Grove Press, 2002.

Edwards, David B. "Before Taliban: Genealogies of the Afghan Jihad." University of California Press, 2002.

"The 9/11 Commission Report." Washington, D.C.: U.S. Government Printing Office, Official Government Edition.

British Broadcasting Corporation – BBC (www.bbc.co.uk).

Christian Science Monitor (www.csmonitor.com).

The (London) Times (www.timesonline.co.uk).

U.S. Department of State (www.state.gov) "Annual Report on International Religious Freedom for 1999: Afghanistan."

Rabin, Yitzhak

Horovitz, David (Editor). "Shalom, Friend – The Life and Legacy of Yitzhak Rabin Memoirs." University of California Press, 1979.

Kort, Michael G. "Yitzhak Rabin – Israel's Soldier Statesman." Brookfield, Connecticut: The Millbrook Press, 1996.

Kurzman, Dan. "Soldier Of Peace – The Life Of Yitzhak Rabin." HarperCollins Publishers, 1998.

Rabin, Leah. "Rabin – Our Life, His Legacy." New York: G.P. Putnam's Sons, 1997.

Rabin, Yitzhak. "The Rabin Memoirs." University of California Press, 1979.

Rizal, José

Arruda, Suzanne Middendorf. "Freedom's Martyr: The Story Of José Rizal, National Hero Of The Philippines." Greensboro, North Carolina: Avisson Press, 2003.

University of Vienna (www.univie.ac.at).

Sadat, Anwar el-

Israeli, Raphael (with Bardenstein, Carol). "Man Of Defiance: A Political Biography Of Anwar Sadat." Barnes & Noble Books, 1985.

Kras, Sara Louis. "Major World Leaders: Anwar Sadat." Chelsea House Publishers, 2003.

Lippman, Thomas W. "Egypt After Nasser." New York: Paragon House, 1989.

Rosen, Deborah Nodler. "Anwar el-Sadat: Middle East Peacemaker." Chicago: Childrens Press, 1986.

Sadat, Anwar el-. "Those I Have Known." New York: The Continuum Publishing Company, 1984.

Sadat, Jehan. "A Woman Of Egypt." New York: Simon And Schuster, 1987.

Scholl, Sophie

Jens, Inge (editor). "At The Heart Of The White Rose." Harper & Row, 1984.

The History Place™ (www.historyplace.com) "Memories Of The White Rose" by George J. Wittenstein, M.D., a survivor of the resistance group The White Rose, 1997.

Wallace, William

Mackay, James. "William Wallace: Brave Heart." Edinburgh and London: Mainstream Publishing, 1995.

Morton, Graeme. "William Wallace: Man and Myth." Sutton Publishing, 2001.

Wallenberg, Raoul

Board, Kjersti (translator). "Letters And Dispatches 1924-1944 Raoul Wallenberg." New York: Arcade Publishing, 1995.

Lester, Elenore. "Wallenberg: The Man In The Iron Web." Englewood Cliffs, New Jersey: Prentice-Hall, Inc., 1982.

McArthur, Debra. "Raoul Wallenberg: Rescuing Thousands from the Nazis' Grasp." Berkeley Heights, New Jersey: Enslow Publishers, 2005.

Nicholson, Michael and Winner, David. "Raoul Wallenberg." Milwaukee: Gareth Stevens Publishing, 1989.

Rosenfeld, Harvey. "Raoul Wallenberg: Angel Of Rescue." Buffalo, New York: Prometheus Books, 1982.

Skoglund, Elizabeth R. "A Quiet Courage: Per Anger, Wallenberg's Co-Liberator of Hungarian Jews." Grand Rapids, Michigan: Baker Books, 1997.

Sudoplatov, Pavel and Anatoli. "Special Tasks: The Memoirs Of An Unwanted Witness – A Soviet Spymaster." Little Brown and Company, 1994.

Werbell, Frederick E. and Clarke, Thurston. "Lost Hero: The Mystery of Raoul Wallenberg." McGraw-Hill Book Company, 1982.

American Jewish Committee (www.ajc.org), an international think tank and advocacy organization, "The Wallenberg Mystery: 55 Years Later" by William Korey.

Minneapolis Star Tribune (16 February 1997) "50 Years After War, Sweden Confronts Troubling Questions."

New York Times Magazine (30 March 1980). "The Lost Hero of the Holocaust: The Search for Sweden's Raoul Wallenberg" by Elenore Lester and Frederick E. Werbell.

U.S. News and World Report (13 May 1996). "The Angel Was a Spy. New Evidence: Sweden's Raoul Wallenberg was a U.S. Espionage Asset."

Zapata, Emiliano

McLynn, Frank. "Villa And Zapata." New York: Carroll & Graf Publishers, 2000.

Ragan, John David. "Emiliano Zapata." Chelsea House Publishers, 1989.

Shorris, Earl. "The Life And Times Of Mexico." New York: W.W. Norton & Company, 2004.

Stein, R. Conrad. "Emiliano Zapata: Revolutionary And Champion Of Poor Farmers." Minnesota: The Child's World, 2004.

Womack, John (translator). "Zapata and the Mexican Revolution." New York: Knopf, 1969.

INDEX

Afghanistan, 298-305, 307-310, 314-315

Allies / Allied Forces, 6, 44, 132-133, 140-141, 147, 169, 199, 236

Al-Qaida, 303, 309, 311-313

Anger, Per, 136, 143, 148

Anglican, 40

Anti-Semitic, 54, 130, 203

Arab, 168, 176, 199, 203, 208-209, 223, 237-238, 243-245, 270, 273, 276, 278-279, 312-313

Arafat, Yassir, 290-291

Arc, Joan of, 23-28, 318

Argentina, 155-156

Arrow Cross, 140-141, 146

Austria / Austrian, 58, 108-117, 135, 139

Axis, 133

Banning, 217, 285

Baroness, 141

Battle, 13, 15, 17-18, 22, 44, 68, 77-78, 83, 97, 236, 278-279, 284

Begin, Menachem, 244-246

Belgium, 41-45, 47-48

Bergman, Ingrid, 172-174

Besnyö, Eva, 160

Biko, Stephen Bantu, 213-221, 318

Birkenhead, Lord, 102

Black and Tans, 97-98

Black Consciousness, 214-216

Black Saturday, 234

Bloody Sunday, 57-58, 97

Boycott, 123, 185-187, 251

Bracken, Josephine, 36, 38

Broadcasting / Television, 115-116, 205-206, 210, 238, 258, 277, 306

Buddhism / Buddhist, 262, 308

Cairo Gang, 97

Camp David Accords, 244-246

Capa, Robert, 158-180, 318

Capitalism, 107

Carranza, Venustiano, 80-82, 84, 87

Carter, Jimmy, 242-244, 246

Catholic, 27, 42, 89, 104-105, 112, 117

Cavell, Eddy, 41, 47

Cavell, Edith, 40-49, 318

Christian, 120, 122, 130, 181, 185, 187-188, 191, 202-203, 222-223, 245, 262, 304

Christian Social Party, 110

Christmas, 16, 41, 48, 94, 146, 222

Churchill, Winston, 102, 104

CIA, 150, 313

Civil Disobedience, 61, 250-251, 255

Civil War, Austrian, 114

Civil War, French, 24

Civil War, Irish, 104-105

Civil War, Pakistan, 260

Civil War, Spanish, 165, 168

Clinton, Bill, 290-292

Cohen, Rosa, 268

Collins, Michael, 89-107, 318

Colonial/Colonialism, 35, 250, 258

Communist, 58, 63, 65, 113, 191, 300-301

Congress Party, 251-252, 254, 258, 262, 265

Conscription, 14, 16

Craig, James, 103-104

Culture, 91, 199, 201, 215, 223, 230, 253-254, 300, 311, 315, 320

Dauphin Charles, 24

Death, 2, 4-5, 7, 13, 19, 26-27, 37-38, 46-47, 49, 54, 63, 79, 84-85, 105, 117, 125, 135, 137, 140, 144-145, 157, 166, 172-173, 179, 204, 210, 219-221, 247-248, 265-266, 272-273, 277, 280, 307, 319

Death March, 144

Debt Slaves, 72-73

Denmark, 151

Divorce, 225, 228-229

Dollfuss, Engelbert, 108-118

Dream Speech, 189-190

Dungeon, 7-9

Easter Rising, 92, 97

Education, 31-33, 51, 81, 120-121, 124, 129, 156, 181-183, 198, 200, 210, 215, 223, 253, 258, 267, 270, 319

Egypt / Egyptian, 206, 222-226, 229-231, 233-247, 277-278, 280, 284, 292-293, 318

Eichmann, Adolf, 135, 137-138, 144, 155-156

Eisenhower, Dwight, 236

Embargo, 209

England / Great Britain, 2-3, 6, 8, 15, 18-19, 21, 40, 42-43, 47-48, 89-90, 97, 102-103, 132, 153, 234, 251, 256

Episcopal, 108

Execution, 20, 26, 38, 46-47, 117, 125, 156, 286, 307, 318

Famine, 23, 110

Fascism, 110

Fatherland Front, 113, 117

Firing Squad, 37-38, 84, 86

Flu Pandemic, 85

France, 18, 23-24, 27, 92, 132, 153, 163, 169, 236, 286, 309

FSB, 149, 154

Gallows, 17

Gandhi, Feroze, 253-258

Gandhi, Indira, 249-267, 319

Gandhi, Mahatma, 187, 250, 253

Gandhi, Rajiv, 256, 265

Gandhi, Sonia, 265

George, David Lloyd, 102

Germany, 54, 58, 61, 111-112, 119-121, 130-133, 149-150, 153-155, 160-161, 200, 256, 272, 286

Ghetto, 132, 145

Gorbachov, Mikhail, 154
Great Cause, 2-3
Griffith, Arthur, 102, 104
Haas, Ernest, 175-176
Hacienda, 71-72, 74-75, 77-78, 86
Haganah, 269, 271-272, 274
Heimwehr, 112-113, 116
Heresy, 25
Hijackers, 286-287, 314
Hindu, 255, 257, 262-263, 265
Hitler, Adolf, 64, 111, 119-120, 124-125, 161, 168, 203, 272
Holocaust, 134, 155-156, 272-273
Holy Communion, 25, 38
Hood, Robin, 5
Huerta, Victoriano, 78-80
Human Rights Abuses, 78, 153, 298, 303, 305
Hungary, 134-136, 141, 148, 153, 158, 318
Igoe Gang, 96

India, 187, 249-251, 254-257, 260-265
Indians, 69, 72, 250-251
Indochina, 168, 177, 179
International Red Cross, 43-44, 138, 143, 146, 171, 240
Iran, 208, 255, 298
Ireland, 89-92, 94, 100, 102-104, 106
Irish Republican Army, 96-97, 100, 104-105
Irish Republican Brotherhood, 90-92
Irish Volunteers, 91-92, 94, 97
Islamic, 198-199, 211, 265, 299, 301, 304-305, 312, 315
Israel / Israeli, 130, 151, 153, 155-156, 168, 176-177, 202, 204, 208-209, 236-245, 247, 268-269, 275-288, 290-292, 294-296, 317
Issat, Hassan, 226-227, 230
Italy, 9, 111, 133, 142
Jackson, Jesse, 193

Japan / Japanese, 38, 132-133, 164, 168, 177, 209

Jewish, 50, 54, 112, 122-123, 127, 130-135, 138, 140, 145, 147-148, 150, 155-156, 158, 176, 202-203, 240, 243, 245, 268-269, 271-272, 274, 276, 279, 284, 286, 292

Jogiches, Leo, 51-55, 58-61, 65

Johnson, Lyndon, 190, 192, 280-282

Jordan, 237, 245, 278-279, 290, 292-293

Kautsky, Costia, 60-61

Kenya, 286-287

KGB, 149, 154

Kibbutz, 271, 274-275

Kiernan, Kitty, 100-102, 105-106

King Abdul, 198-199, 201-202, 204

King Alexander, 2

King Edward, 1-3, 5-6, 17, 21

King Faisal, 198-212, 240, 318

King John, 3, 6, 18

King Jr., Martin Luther, 181-197, 319

King Saud, 204-206

King, Coretta Scott, 184, 191

Kissinger, Henry, 241, 247, 283

Laden, Osama bin, 303, 307-309, 312

Land Reform, 67, 74, 79, 82-83

Lantos, Tom and Annette, 153

Lauer, Koloman, 133-134, 137

Lawson, Rev. James, 194

Leader / Leadership, 9, 58, 63, 76, 79-81, 84, 86, 89, 92, 94, 102, 110, 112, 114, 116, 118, 126, 160, 188, 191-192, 194, 203, 206-207, 214, 216-217, 243-245, 247, 259, 262, 272-273, 275, 290, 301, 305, 317-320

Legends, 5, 305

Legacy, 179, 181, 211, 265, 296, 315

Lion of Panjshir, 279-298, 301-302, 308, 310, 314-315

Lithuania, 54

Luxemburg, Rosa, 50-66, 319

Madero, Francisco, 74, 76, 78

Magnum, 174-177, 179

Maid of Norway, 2

Marion, 12-13

Marriage / Wedding, 2, 12, 33, 36-38, 41, 54-55, 60, 73, 101, 105, 108, 131, 167, 173, 223-224, 228-233, 254-255, 299

Mass, 16, 26, 102, 114

Massood, Ahmad Shah, 298-316

Meir, Golda, 243, 269, 283

Menteith, Sir John de, 19

Mestizo, 68

Mexico, 67-88

Middle East, 203, 208, 222, 239-240, 245

Monkey Brigade, 252-253

Montaño, Otilio, 75, 81, 84

Mubarak, Hosni, 292

Muslim, 199, 203, 205, 211, 222, 228, 232 245, 247, 257, 300-301, 304-305, 309

Mussolini, Benito, 111

Nasser, Gamal Abdel, 224, 233, 238-239, 277

Nazis / Nazi Party, 111-123, 126, 130, 132-136, 140, 143, 150-151, 153, 161, 203, 256, 292

Negotiations, 52, 101-103, 114, 209, 243, 245, 286, 290

Netherlands, 45

Nixon, Richard, 208-209, 238-239, 260, 283, 285

Nobel Prize, 151, 190-191, 245-246, 290

Norway, 2, 191, 245, 290

Nuremberg, 131, 155

Obregón, Ávaro, 87

Occupation, 14, 96, 149, 230, 301-302

Oil, 200-201, 204, 208-209, 240, 242

Omar, Mawlawi Mohammed, 303, 305
Operation Entebbe, 286-287
Oppression, 33, 89, 107, 214
Oppressor, 9, 20, 133
Pakistan, 257, 260-261, 298, 300-301, 303, 311
Palestine, 130-131, 154, 176, 202-203, 268-270, 272, 276, 285, 289
Palmach, 271, 273-275, 277
Parks, Rosa, 185
Passport, 44, 54, 128, 136, 141, 143, 154, 173
Patriotism / Patriots, 8, 14, 89, 106, 113, 226
Peace Rally, 293
Peace Talks / Treaty, 101-102, 105, 114, 246-247, 290-291
Peres, Shimon, 290-291, 293, 296
Phantom Jets, 282-283, 287
Philippines, 29-30, 32, 35-36, 38-39

Photography, 160-161, 165-166, 172, 179-180
Plan Of Ayala, 74-75, 80-81
Poland, 50-53, 58, 123, 132, 143, 318
Poppies, 307-308
Prison, 6, 9, 25, 30, 36-37, 46, 55-56, 59-61, 63-64, 92-94, 96, 105, 109, 125, 149, 151-154, 156, 163, 195, 216, 218, 224-226, 228-229, 233, 253, 255, 261, 286-87, 295, 318
Probst, Christoph, 125
Quran, 223, 229-230, 304, 306
Rabin, Leah, 274-275, 277, 282, 288, 293-296
Rabin, Yitzhak, 243, 268-297, 317
Ramadan, 227, 229
Rebels, 37, 73, 77-80, 93
Revolution, 35-37, 62-63, 65, 93, 95, 124, 133, 160, 224, 234
Revolution, Mexican, 73-74, 78, 80, 83-84, 87
Rivera, Leonor, 33

Rizal, José, 29-39, 319
Robert the Bruce, 3, 6, 18, 21
Robichov, Nehemiah, 268
Roosevelt, Franklin Delano, 134, 201-202
Russia / Russian, 50, 57-59, 123, 129, 146-151, 153-154, 160, 236, 268, 315
Sadat, Anwar el-, 222-248, 318-319
Sadat, Jehan, 226-233, 240
Saint(s), 23-24, 26-27
Saudi Arabia, 198-201, 204-208, 240, 303, 310, 318
Scholl, Hans, 121-122, 124-125
Scholl, Sophie, 119-126, 319
Schutz-Pass, 135-138, 142-143
Scotland, 1-4, 6, 8-9, 12-13, 15-16, 18, 21
Shariah, 199, 304
Sikhs, 262-266
Sinn Féin, 93-94, 96-97

Six-Day War, 237-239, 243, 277, 280-281
Social Democracy, 52, 59, 61-62, 113-114
Socialist, 63, 125
Solomon's Temple, 269, 279
South Africa, 129-130, 213-219, 221, 258
Spain, 29, 32-33, 36, 39, 165-166, 168
Spartacus League, 62-63
Spies / Spy, 45, 95, 97-99, 104, 149, 154, 252
Stock Market Crash, 110, 159
Sudan, 222, 303
Suez Canal, 201, 234-235, 237, 241, 284
Suez War, 236
Sweden, 127-128, 130, 133-135, 137-138, 151
Swedish Legation, 134-136, 143, 148
Switzerland, 51, 54, 138, 153, 254, 286
Syria, 237, 240, 279, 284
Taliban, 303-305, 307-309, 311-312, 314-315

Taro, Gerda, 161-169, 172

Terrorists, 247, 263, 286-287, 308

Thunayan, Iffat al-, 200

Trial, 19, 25, 27, 36-37, 61-62, 99, 117, 125-126, 141, 156, 226, 233, 251, 255

Truman, Harry, 204

Turkey, 128, 200

Twelve Apostles, 96

U.S. Government, 79, 93, 290

Uganda, 286-287

United Nations, 201, 203, 219, 241, 276-277, 307-308

United States, 38-39, 68, 79-80, 101, 129-130, 132, 154, 163, 173-174, 208-210, 219, 236-239, 242, 268, 271, 282, 288, 301, 303, 311, 313-314

Ustinov, Peter, 264

Valera, Eamon de, 102, 104

Villa, Pancho, 73, 79-82, 84

Wahhabi, 204

Wallace, William, 1-22, 319

Wallenberg, Raoul Gustav, 127-157, 318-319

War Refugee Board, 134

White Rose, The, 121-125

Wiesenthal, Simon, 153

Wilson, Woodrow, 79

World War I, 43, 47, 61-63, 91-92, 109, 112, 114, 119, 128, 199, 203, 268

World War II, 127, 132-133, 155, 168-169, 174, 176, 200, 203, 209, 256, 271, 276

Yeltsin, Boris, 154

Yom Kippur War, 239, 246, 284

Yugoslavia, 239-240

Zapata, Emiliano, 67-88

Zapatistas, 76-79, 81-83, 86-87

Zion / Zionist, 132, 203, 243, 268-269, 279, 292, 296

ORDER FORM

(For the current form or to pay by credit card or PayPal, go to: www.susanv.com)

Use this form to pay by money order or company/personal check, made <u>payable to: Bootheel Publishing</u>. Orders will be filled after check clears.

<u>Postal Mail:</u>

Bootheel Publishing

P.O. Box 6

Fenton, MO 63026 U.S.A.

<u>SHIP TO (Continental U.S. Only):</u>

Name: _____

Address: _____

City: _____ State: _____

Zip: _____ Phone: _____

E-mail: _____

Send: "Legends, Leaders, Legacies"

Book cost:	$_____
Sales tax Missouri only:	$_____
Shipping and handling	$_____
Subtotal:	$_____
Grand total: (Subtotal _____ x Quantity ____)	$_____

❑ Autograph this copy at no extra charge to the attention of: _____.

❑ No autograph needed. (Note: If no box is checked, book will "not" be signed.)

<u>Form updated: 2 April 2007</u>

ORDER FORM

(For the current form or to pay by credit card or PayPal, go to: www.susanv.com)

Use this form to pay by money order or company/personal check, made payable to: Bootheel Publishing. Orders will be filled after check clears.

Postal Mail:

Bootheel Publishing

P.O. Box 6

Fenton, MO 63026 U.S.A.

SHIP TO (Continental U.S. Only):

Name: _____

Address: _____

City: _____ **State:** _____

Zip: _____ **Phone:** _____

E-mail: _____

Send: "Legends, Leaders, Legacies"

Book cost:	$_____
Sales tax Missouri only:	$_____
Shipping and handling	$_____
Subtotal:	$_____
Grand total: (Subtotal _____ x Quantity ____)	$_____

- ❏ Autograph this copy at no extra charge to the attention of: _____.
- ❏ No autograph needed. (Note: If no box is checked, book will "not" be signed.)

<u>Form updated: 2 April 2007</u>

Printed in the United States
81851LV00002B/253-312